DO NOT REMOVE
CARDS FROM POCKET

Freedom
of Expression

FREEDOM OF EXPRESSION

The Right
to Speak Out
in America

Elaine Pascoe

Issue and Debate

The Millbrook Press
Brookfield, Connecticut

For Moriarty

Photographs courtesy of Library of Congress: pp. 10, 18, 23, 29,
37; Bettmann Archive: pp. 20, 83; Sophia Smith Collection, Smith
College, Northampton, Mass.: p. 34; UPI/Bettmann: pp. 45, 53, 66,
97, 100; AP/World Wide Photos: pp. 56, 80; Rothco: pp. 59, 69, 88;
American Library Association: p. 105; Ginger Giles: p. 111.

Library of Congress Cataloging-in-Publication Data
Pascoe, Elaine
Freedom of expression : the right to speak out in America / by Elaine Pascoe.
p. cm. — (Issue and debate)
Includes bibliographical references and index.
Summary: Traces the First Amendment's roots in earlier societies, and exam-
ines how it has been tested and interpreted from colonial times to the present.
ISBN 1-56294-255-7
1. Freedom of speech—United States—Juvenile literature. [1. Freedom of
speech. 2. United States—Constitutional law—Amendments—1st-10th.]
I. Title. II. Series.
KF4772.Z9P37 1992
342.73'0853—DC20 92-7150 [347.302853] CIP AC

Published by The Millbrook Press
2 Old New Milford Road
Brookfield, Connecticut 06804

Contents

*They that can give up essential liberty
to obtain a little temporary safety deserve
neither liberty nor safety.*

Benjamin Franklin

Freedom
of Expression

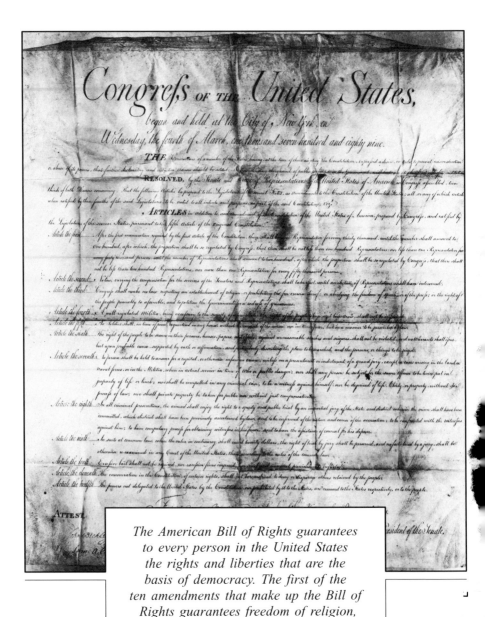

The American Bill of Rights guarantees
to every person in the United States
the rights and liberties that are the
basis of democracy. The first of the
ten amendments that make up the Bill of
Rights guarantees freedom of religion,
speech, assembly, and petition.

A Bedrock Principle

On a warm summer day in 1984, about a hundred demonstrators gathered in front of City Hall in Dallas, Texas, to protest the Republican National Convention, which was being held in that city. It was a scene that for the United States, with its traditions of open political debate and freedom of expression, was completely unremarkable—until one of the demonstrators, Gregory Lee Johnson, unfurled an American flag, doused it with kerosene, and set it on fire. As the Stars and Stripes went up in smoke and flames, the group chanted, "America, the red, white, and blue, we spit on you."[1]

Johnson was promptly arrested for violating a Texas law that prohibited desecration of the flag. He was convicted, fined $2,000, and sentenced to a year in prison. But that was only the beginning of his story. Johnson brought his case to the Texas Court of Criminal Appeals, which overturned his conviction. The state then appealed to the United States Supreme Court.

In 1989, five years after Johnson had set a match to the flag, the Supreme Court issued its ruling in the case of *Texas* v. *Johnson*. Laws that prohibited flag burning as a political protest, the Court said, were unconstitutional because burning the flag was a form of speech, or expression—and as such was protected by the First Amendment to the Constitution. Justice William J. Brennan, in the majority opinion, wrote: "If there is a bedrock principle underlying the First Amendment, it is that the Government may not prohibit the expression of an idea simply because society finds the idea itself offensive or disagreeable."[2]

Johnson touched off a storm of debate. Even the Supreme Court was divided, 5–4, in its ruling, with strong dissenting opinions delivered by Chief Justice William H. Rehnquist and several other justices. Yet Johnson's act was only one of several events that in recent years have put the concept of freedom of expression at the center of national controversy. News broadcasts, advertisements, works of art, the lyrics of songs, the content of books on library shelves, and even clothing have become the center of sharp, often heated debate.

The First Amendment states with elegant simplicity: "Congress shall make no law . . . abridging the freedom of speech, or of the press." But the simplicity is deceptive. Despite the amendment's blanket ban on laws curtailing expression, people in the United States are not free to say or publish anything they choose. There are limits, and few people would argue that some restrictions aren't necessary—that it would be all right, for example, to publish troop locations or battle plans in wartime. The question is, What should the limits be?

Moreover, the concept of speech itself is fluid and hard to define. Generally, the First Amendment is held to protect forms of expression that go beyond printed or spoken words—works of art, for example, or actions such as flag burning. But the question of exactly which forms of "speech" are protected and which are not is debated.

As a rule, it has fallen to courts and legal scholars to answer these questions. And at different times, they have found various answers. In one view, the First Amendment's protection of speech is absolute. Justice Hugo L. Black, who served on the Supreme Court from 1937 to 1971, wrote that the government "is without any power whatever under the Constitution to put any type of burden on speech and expression of ideas of any kind"—in other words, when the First Amendment says "no law," it means, literally, "no law."[3] However, even Black placed some limits on expression. He drew a distinction between speech and action, which he believed should not be protected to the same extent.

In another view, freedom of expression is just one of several rights and ideals enshrined in the Constitution and, as such, should be weighed and balanced against the others. Speech might be curtailed, for example, if it would prevent a criminal defendant from receiving a fair trial, another constitutionally protected right. Some people who have taken this view would give the First Amendment primacy; that is, they would weight it more heavily than other rights. Others would not.

A third view sees the First Amendment protecting primarily political speech—the debate on public affairs that is necessary in a democracy—but offering only limited protection in other areas. There have been other interpretations as well.

In part, the difficulty in deciding just what the First Amendment means stems from the fact that no one is sure what, exactly, its authors intended. Along with the other nine amendments that make up the Bill of Rights, it was hammered out in closed-door committee meetings by members of the First Congress in 1789. Clearly, too, the authors could not have predicted the many situations in which the amendment has been invoked since then— situations involving everything from the disclosure of government secrets to rap lyrics.

But the authors of the First Amendment did make their views on free speech known. And the concept of freedom of expression has a long history; it is an idea that has evolved over centuries. Thus the search for answers in today's debates begins in the past.

2

A Right
Secured

In 421 B.C., during the twilight of the Golden Age of Athens, the Greek playwright Euripides wrote:

This is true liberty, when free-born men,
Having to advise the public, may speak free,
Which he who can and will, deserves high praise;
Who neither can nor will, may hold his peace;
What can be juster in a State than this?[1]

Even at its height, Athens was not a haven of free expression. (Significantly, the philosopher Socrates was sentenced to death for "corrupting" the youth of Athens with his teaching.) But Euripides' statement shows that the Athenians, to whom the founders of the United States looked with admiration, at least recognized a basic principle: Open debate is essential in a democracy.

The concept of freedom of expression did not gain much ground in the ancient world, however. In fact, in the more than two thousand years that passed between the Golden Age of Athens and the writing of the First

Amendment, it fared badly. A catalog of instances in which speech was suppressed would fill volumes. Among the more notable examples, the Catholic Church exercised rigorous censorship throughout most of Europe during the Middle Ages. Beginning in the 1200s, heretics (those whose religious views differed from official church doctrine) were pursued by the Inquisition, a church tribunal that had the power to sentence them to death.

Free Speech in England. England was spared the worst effects of the Inquisition, but speech was severely restricted there as well. In the 1400s, speaking or writing anything critical of the king or his ministers was considered sedition, or undermining the authority of the state—a crime that could be punished by imprisonment or even, for repeat offenders, death.

The printing press, introduced into England in 1476, created new concerns because printed material could be widely distributed. The government tried to control the situation by licensing presses and books, so that nothing could be printed without the approval of royal officials. From 1487 through 1641, these controls were exercised largely by the infamous Star Chamber, a court of high-ranking government officials that heard cases behind closed doors and meted out punishments that included fines, imprisonment, and even splitting noses and cutting off ears.

The 1500s and 1600s were turbulent years in England. In the 1500s, the English king Henry VIII broke away from the Catholic Church and established the Church of England, with himself as its head. This began a long period of political and religious conflict. The stakes for speaking out against the government were raised considerably—such speech could be considered treason and punished by death. Moreover, it was a crime not only to speak or write against the government but merely to possess a book or pamphlet that did so.

Such laws did not stop the spread of new ideas, however. The 1600s brought growing conflict between the monarchy, which saw its power as absolute, and the English Parliament. Civil war broke out in 1642, during the reign of Charles I. Charles was forced to give up power; Parliament and its leader, Oliver Cromwell, took control of the country. But the rule of Parliament was far from democratic. Cromwell and his followers were Puritans with strict religious views, and they sought to impose those views on the country. New laws limiting expression were passed.

One of these laws sparked a spirited defense of the principle of free speech—*Areopagitica,** written in 1644 by the poet John Milton. Milton wrote to protest a law that required all books, pamphlets, and other printed materials to be licensed by the government before publication; in the process, he outlined three central arguments that have been used against censorship ever since.

First, Milton wrote, censorship is almost impossible to enforce. Controlling books is like trying to "pound up the crows by shutting the park gate"—people will be exposed to new ideas anyway. Second, open debate encourages knowledge and progress; in fact, the clash of competing ideas itself is a sign that society is moving forward. Finally, given free choice in a "marketplace" of ideas, people are capable of choosing the best: "Though all the winds of doctrine were let loose to play upon the earth, so Truth be in the field, we do injuriously by licensing and prohibiting to misdoubt her strength."[2]

* The title refers to the Areopagus, an ancient Athenian court symbolic of the height of wisdom and democracy in that city.

John Milton, the English poet and political writer, was best known for his epic poetry. His most famous prose work was Areopagitica, *a defense of freedom of the press.*

Despite Milton's eloquence, licensing remained part of English law for another fifty years (and thus applied to England's North American colonies as well). The monarchy was restored, with limited powers, in 1660. The English Bill of Rights, adopted in 1689, provided freedom of speech only for members of Parliament. But the ideas Milton expressed would emerge again, in America as well as in England.

Restrictions in the Colonies. In 1686 a London printer named Benjamin Harris was accused of publishing seditious pamphlets and fled England for America, where he opened a combined book and coffee shop in Boston. Harris's shop soon became a favorite stopping place for some of Boston's leading writers and thinkers, many of whom shared the proprietor's liberal views.

On September 25, 1690, Harris published what some people consider the first newspaper in America, *Publick Occurrences Both Forreign and Domestick.* It included a wide range of reports, from news of a smallpox epidemic, a suicide, and relations with Indians to gossip about the private life of the king of France. Harris intended to bring the newspaper out monthly, or more often if there was "any Glut of Occurrences."[3] But the first issue was also the last—the paper was promptly suppressed by the colonial governor.

Harris had violated licensing restrictions that were first imposed in Massachusetts in 1662. More serious, however, the newspaper made statements that the governor and others found dangerous and offensive; for example, that the Indian allies of the English were "miserable savages, in whom we have too much confided."[4] Harris's career as a publisher was over (he eventually returned to England, where he made a living selling quack medicines), and it would be fourteen years before a regularly

Numb. 1.

PUBLICK
OCCURRENCES

Both *FORREIGN* and *DOMESTICK.*

Boston, Thursday Sept. 25th. 1690.

America is known throughout the world for its liberal policy in regard to freedom of the press. Therefore, it is ironic that what is considered to be America's first newspaper, Publick Occurrences Both Forreign and Domestick, *published only one issue before being closed down by colonial authorities who were offended by its editorial content.*

published newspaper, the *Boston News-Letter,* appeared in America.

Harris was not the last colonial printer to get in trouble for publishing a newspaper. Among the others was James Franklin, older brother of Benjamin Franklin. In 1721 his Boston newspaper the *New-England Courant* began to attack the authorities and some of the city's leading citizens over a newly developed smallpox inoculation, which the authorities approved but which Franklin considered too risky. Soon Franklin was criticizing the government on other grounds as well. He was ordered to stop publication; when he refused, he was jailed. Even then the *New-England Courant* continued to appear—James simply named Benjamin as publisher.

Unlike Harris, Franklin won his fight with the authorities. Formal licensing was no longer in effect, and a grand jury declined to indict him for continuing to publish his newspaper after it was banned. Franklin thus established an important principle in America: that government did not have a blanket right to restrict the press *before* publication.

In fact, this principle was gaining ground in England as well, and by the mid-1700s it was widely accepted. At that time one of England's foremost legal authorities, Sir William Blackstone, wrote:

> *The liberty of the press is indeed essential to the nature of a free state; but this consists in laying no previous restraints upon publications, and not in freedom from censure for criminal matter when published. Every free man has a right to lay what sentiments he pleases before the public . . . but if he publishes what is improper, mischievous or illegal, he must take the consequences.*[5]

In other words, people could be punished after the fact for statements that the government considered seditious or criminal. But this concept, too, came under attack. In America, it was at the core of one of the most important free-speech cases of colonial times, the Zenger trial of 1735.

This case had its roots in a dispute between some of the leading citizens of New York and that colony's governor, William Cosby, who they believed had overstepped his authority, acquired land illegally, and even rigged elections for the colonial council. In 1733, John Peter Zenger, a New York printer, began to publish a newspaper called the *New York Weekly Journal* that was sharply critical of the governor and extremely popular with the public—he had to print extra editions to meet the demand. The governor was not so pleased; he charged Zenger with seditious libel.

Libel is published defamation; that is, a statement that presents a person in a bad light and harms his or her reputation. Seditious libel is defamation that tends to undermine the authority of the state. Under the law as it was then, it was up to the judges in the case to decide if Zenger had defamed Cosby and if this tended to undermine the governor's authority—and in their eyes, there was no question. All that remained for a jury to settle was the cut-and-dry question of whether Zenger had actually printed the material.

Zenger was defended by Andrew Hamilton, an eighty-year-old Philadelphia lawyer with shoulder-length white hair and a formidable reputation. Hamilton stunned the court by acknowledging outright that Zenger had published the defamatory newspapers. He then pursued an argument that was revolutionary for the time: that citizens had a right to criticize the government, as long as their statements were not false or malicious. When the

The 1735 libel trial of John Peter Zenger became a major step in the American colonies' struggle for freedom of the press. A jury found Zenger innocent of the charge of criticizing the British government after his attorney argued that Zenger had printed the truth, and the truth is not libelous.

judges refused to hear this defense, he calmly turned his back on them and presented his argument to the jury:

> *The question before the court and you gentle-*
> *men of the jury, is not of small nor private con-*
> *cern. It is not the cause of the poor printer, nor*
> *of New York alone. . . . It is the best cause. It*
> *is the cause of liberty. . . . Nature and the laws*
> *of our country have given us a right— the lib-*
> *erty—both of exposing and opposing arbitrary*
> *power . . . by speaking and writing—truth.*[6]

The jury found Zenger not guilty. His trial did not imme-diately change the law, but Hamilton's arguments had planted the seeds of several important principles: first, that citizens have a right to criticize government; second, that a true statement can't be considered libel; and third, that a jury has the right to rule on the law, not just the facts of the case before it. It would take time for these ideas to become firmly established; but, as former chief justice William O. Douglas described it, the Zenger case was "a milestone in the fight for the right to criticize the government."[7]

Guaranteeing Free Speech. Harris, Franklin, and Zenger were just three of many people who were dragged into court for written or spoken statements in colonial America. More often than not, it was the colonial legislatures rather than the royal governors that brought charges of seditious libel. And while several of the colonies adopted charters of rights, most of these charters paid little attention to freedom of speech or the press.

Nevertheless, the idea that freedom of expression was a basic human right gained ground steadily in the 1700s. Newspapers such as Zenger's *New York Weekly Journal* and Benjamin Franklin's *Pennsylvania Gazette* reprinted essays on the subject that had appeared in London newspapers under the pseudonym Cato. They described free speech as "the Right of every man, as far as by it he does not hurt or control the Right of another" and "the Symptom as well as the Effect of good Government."[8] These opinions echoed the views of the English philosopher John Locke, who in the late 1600s had put forward the idea that people had certain natural rights and that one of the obligations of government was to protect those rights.

Opponents of British rule in particular took up the banner of free speech. This is hardly surprising, as they were expressing antigovernment opinions. Nor is it surprising that colonial newspapers, which were heavily taxed by the Stamp Act of 1765, firmly advocated press freedom. (But the Patriots, as opponents of British rule were called, often did not think the same rights extended to Tories, who supported Britain. Patriot mobs even smashed some Tory printing presses.)

In 1774, delegates from twelve of the colonies met in Philadelphia in what became known as the First Continental Congress, in a last-ditch effort to avoid an open break with Britain. One of their acts was to issue a declaration of rights that, among other things, set out a basic rationale for freedom of the press:

The importance of this consists, besides the advancement of truth, science, morality and arts in general, in its diffusion of liberal sentiment on the administration of government, its ready communication of thoughts between subjects, and its consequential promotion of union among them, whereby oppressive officials are shamed or intimidated into more honorable and just modes of conducting affairs.[9]

Thus, by the time of the Revolutionary War, three theories of freedom of expression had gained wide acceptance. The first, set out by Milton in *Areopagitica* more than a century before, held that society would be served by a "marketplace of ideas." The second, drawing on the philosophy of Locke, was that freedom of expression was a natural human right. And the third, as stated by the First Continental Congress, was that open debate promoted good government, by keeping citizens informed and providing a check on government officials. All three views would have a strong influence on the events to come.

"What the People Are Entitled To." With the Declaration of Independence and the outbreak of the Revolutionary War, the former colonies were faced with the task of governing themselves. One by one, they adopted constitutions, and eleven of them included charters of rights or other provisions that guaranteed individual liberties. By 1787 nine of the thirteen states had adopted some sort of guarantee of press freedom. However, no such guarantees were offered in the Articles of Confederation, which from 1781 to 1789 provided the framework of the United States government.

That framework soon proved weak indeed. Under the Articles, the power of Congress was so limited that it could not enforce laws or raise enough money to pay the debts (even soldiers' back pay) from the Revolutionary War. Meanwhile, the states acted virtually as independent countries, arguing over boundaries and trade, and the economy of the new country was in tatters. In 1786 a group of debt-ridden Massachusetts farmers, led by Daniel Shays, rebelled. The rebellion was promptly put down, but it sounded an alarm: Clearly, a stronger central authority was needed if the country was to hold together.

In May 1787, delegates from all the states except Rhode Island met in Philadelphia to address the problem. They scrapped the Articles of Confederation and produced, four months later, the Constitution that still governs the United States. It established a strong national government that could raise taxes, enforce laws, keep an army, and exercise other powers without the consent of the states because it would draw its authority directly from the people. To prevent any abuse of power, the authors of the Constitution set up a system of checks and balances, with powers divided among three branches—legislative, executive, and judicial.

But before this Constitution could take effect, the states had to approve it. Many people had deep reservations about the idea of putting so much power in the hands of a national government. Small states worried that large states would dominate the Union. Southern states worried that Northern states would monopolize trade and try to limit slavery. Small farmers worried that large landowners would exercise too much influence. And some people worried that a powerful national government would trample on the individual liberties—including freedom of expression—that had been fought for in the Revolutionary War.

Thomas Jefferson was among those who argued that the Constitution ought to contain guarantees of these liberties—a bill of rights—as many state constitutions did. "A bill of rights is what the people are entitled to against every government on earth . . . and what no government should refuse," he wrote.[10] Taking the other view were the Federalists, led by Alexander Hamilton. The Federalists, who pressed hard for the adoption of the new Constitution, argued that no guarantees were necessary because the document gave the federal government only specific powers. "Bills of rights are, in their origin, stipulations between kings and their subjects, . . . reservations of rights not surrendered to the prince," one Federalist wrote. In the Constitution, "the people surrender nothing; and, as they retain everything, they have no need of particular reservations."[11]

Nonetheless, many state legislatures refused to ratify the Constitution without assurances that a bill of rights would be promptly added to it. Thus, when the first Congress of the new government met in 1789, amending the Constitution was the first order of business. In fact, the Congress was flooded with more than two hundred proposed amendments—some of which would actually have limited civil liberties.

The ten amendments that emerged as the Bill of Rights were shaped largely by James Madison. Madison had originally been neutral on the idea of a charter of rights. "I have never thought the omission a material defect, nor been anxious to supply it even by *subsequent* amendment, for any other reason than that it is anxiously desired by others," he wrote to Jefferson in 1788.[12] But he came to see it as important in its own right, as well as a way of securing the approval of reluctant states.

Madison argued with special eloquence for protection of freedom of speech and of the press, which he listed among the "great rights." In fact, among the amendments he proposed was one that would have prevented state governments, not only Congress, from violating "the equal rights of conscience, or of the freedom of the press . . . because it is proper that every Government should be disarmed of powers which trench upon those particular rights." He argued, "I cannot see any reason against obtaining even a double security on these points."[13] The House of Representatives added freedom of speech to this amendment and passed it, but it failed

*James Madison is credited with shaping
the Bill of Rights. He argued especially
strongly for the First Amendment, and he
became a leading advocate for its
ratification by the states.*

to win the necessary two-thirds majority in the Senate. At that time, senators were elected by the state legislatures, and the state legislatures felt that they were already giving up too many powers to the federal government.

Still, Madison was satisfied by the wording that finally appeared in the First Amendment. "We shall find that the censorial power is in the people over the Government and not in the Government over the people," he wrote confidently in 1794.[14]

3

Political
Speech

Madison was perhaps too optimistic. Within four years of his statement, the government passed a pair of the most repressive laws in U.S. history. The Alien and Sedition Acts, approved by Congress in the summer of 1798, were a direct attempt by the political party in power to silence its opponents, and they provided the new United States with the first major test of its commitment to the principle of free speech in the political arena.

The laws were very much a product of their time—a time marked by bitter and sometimes violent partisan politics. Much of the most heated political debate focused on the new country's relations with Britain and France, who were then at war. The Federalists—the party of George Washington and of John Adams, who was elected president in 1796—tended to support Britain. The Anti-Federalists took up the French cause.

Both sides aired the dispute in the press. Newspapers of the time made no pretense of objective reporting; they were blatantly partisan, and many were financed by political groups. In a typical exchange, the Anti-Federalist editor Benjamin Franklin Bache (a grandson of Benjamin Franklin), who published the *Aurora* in Philadelphia, wrote: "If ever a nation was debauched by a man, the American nation has been debauched by Washington."[1] In response, a Federalist mob whipped Bache in public and wrecked the newspaper office.

A number of incidents swung public opinion against the French and in favor of the Federalist position. (Among them was the XYZ Affair, in which the French foreign minister allegedly demanded a bribe before agreeing to meet with American diplomats.) By the time John Adams took office, the United States was on the point of war with France. It was this climate that produced the Alien and Sedition Acts. The laws allowed the president to deport "subversive" foreigners and mandated fines and up to two years in prison for any person who "shall write, print, utter, or publish . . . any false, scandalous and malicious writing . . . against the government of the United States."[2]

The Federalists promptly began to use the laws to muzzle their opponents—but the action backfired. There were only ten convictions, but they were so obviously partisan that they provoked a public outcry. Opposition to the laws helped win support for Thomas Jefferson's Democratic-Republican party, and Jefferson won the presidential election of 1800. The furor also advanced the theory of freedom of expression. Among those who spoke out against the act was the lawyer and politician George Hay, who was one of the first to argue that speech could not be limited in any way. Hay wrote:

The word "freedom" has meaning. It is either absolute, that is, exempt from all law, or it is qualified, that is, regulated by law. . . . If it is to be regulated by law, the Amendment which declared that Congress shall make no law to abridge the freedom of the press . . . is the grossest absurdity that ever was conceived by the human mind.[3]

Few people shared Hay's view, however. Although Congress debated the matter, the Alien and Sedition Acts were not repealed. Rather, they were simply allowed to expire in March 1801, and those who had been jailed were pardoned.

Jefferson was viciously attacked in the press during his term and (as he confessed in a letter to a friend) was tempted to bring action against several Federalist editors, but he remained convinced of the benefit of freedom of expression. Of the Federalists, he wrote in 1802, "I shall protect them in the right of lying . . . by pursuing steadily my object of proving that a people . . . are capable of conducting themselves under a government founded not on the fears and follies of man, but on his reason."[4]

Free Speech and the Slavery Debate. It would be more than a century before the federal government, during World War I, would again impose laws against "sedition." But that did not mean that the United States entered a golden age of freedom of expression. On the contrary, nothing prevented states from enacting laws that limited expression, and many did. Political opinions were often expressed at the speaker's (or printer's) peril during the 1800s.

This was especially the case in the years leading up to the Civil War, when slavery became the most hotly debated issue in the country. Most Southern states passed laws that barred any criticism of slavery, on the theory that speaking against it would incite revolts. In some

THE LIBERATOR.

Our Country is the World, our Countrymen are all Mankind.

NO. 28.   BOSTON, FRIDAY, JULY 8, 1864.   W

...incoln personally responsible. I hold him respon-
ble for all the waste of treasure—all the waste of
precious life during the last two years. (Applause.)
With a man at the head of the government, a man
who knew how not merely to manage parties, to play
off one clique against another, a man who under-
stood the people and had sympathy with them, who
had a soul that could kindle up the souls of others,
draw out the spirit of the people, concentrate and
direct it against the rebellion—that rebellion would
ave been put down in the year 1861. (Applause.)
There is no use of deceiving ourselves about it.

LETTER OF WENDELL PHILLIPS.

Wendell Phillips's very remarkable letter on the
approaching presidential canvass will attract widespread attention both from the novelty and boldness
of the views, as well as for the force and point with
which they are presented. The great abolitionist
sees and acknowledges that the country will be
ruined if Lincoln is reelected, and the present administration continued in power, and he is, moreover,
fairly compelled to own that the hope of the nation
is in the Democratic party. He calls for an honest
union of all the elements of opposition to Lincoln,
to save the country from the calamity of another
four years of such administration as we now suffer
from. Wendell Phillips is usually erratic, crotch-
ty, and unreliable, but the letter we quote else-
where contains more common sense than the whole
volume of his recently published abolition diatribes.
—New York World.

The letter here approvingly referred to by this
copperhead journal, (which combines in itself the
scriptural trinity described as "the World, the Flesh,
and the Devil,") is the one we print in another column.
Adressed to the Editor of the New York Independent,
the World puts the following caption to the letter :

OLEVELAND VERSUS BALTIMORE.

Wendell Phillips writes a Stinging Letter on the
Baltimore Platform—its Clap-trap Compliments
to Lincoln—an Administration which shows
vigor only in Peaceful Cities—a Government feared only by its Loyal
Citizens—"The Union well-
nigh Wrecked."

Selections.

THE PRESIDENTIAL NOMINATION.

The correspondence between the Committee of
the National Union Convention and President Lincoln, including the official notification of the President's nomination and his letter of acceptance, was
as follows :—

NEW YORK, June 14, 1864.

Hon. Abraham Lincoln :
Sir : The National Union Convention, which as-
sembled in Baltimore on the 7th of June, 1864, has
instructed us to inform you that you were nominat-
ed with enthusiastic unanimity for the Presidency
of the United States, for four years from the 4th of
March next.

The resolutions of the Convention, which we
have already had the honor of placing in your
hands, are a full and clear statement of the principles which inspired its action, and which, as we believe, the great body of Union men in the country
heartily approve. Whether those resolutions express the national gratitude to our soldiers and sail-
ors, or the national scorn of compromise with reb-
els, and consequent dishonor, or the patriotic duty
of union and success ; whether they approve the
Proclamation of Emancipation, the Constitutional
amendment, the employment of former slaves as
Union soldiers, or the solemn obligation of the Government promptly to redress the wrongs of every
soldier of the Union of whatever color or race ;
whether they declare the inviolability of the
pledged faith of the nation, or offer the national hospi-
tality to the oppressed of every land, or urge the
union by railroad of the Atlantic and Pacific
Oceans ; whether they recommend public economy

THE LATE HON. JOSHUA R. GIDDINGS.

We give below the remarks of Rev. Mr. Cordner,
at a meeting held in Montreal, for the purpose of passing resolutions, expressing the high regard of the citizens for the admirable qualities of the character of
the late Hon. Joshua R. Giddings, Consul-General of
the United States to Canada, and their appreciation
"of his great services in the cause of human rights by
his active and consistent opposition to slavery throughout a lengthened public career." The Mayor of the
city presided, and many prominent gentlemen were
present, and spoke feelingly of the public loss which
had been sustained in the death of Mr. Giddings.

Mr. Cordner, in moving the first of a series of resolutions, said the call of the Hon. J. R. Giddings
from amongst them by sudden death, had come as a
sad surprise to all who had the privilege in any degree of his personal acquaintance. The necessarily
prompt removal, too, of his remains had caused dis-
appointment, and led to a wish for some public testimony of regard to his memory ; hence the present
meeting to declare their respect for his consistency,
and long indomitable championship of the primal
rights of man, be he black or white. Although
called away suddenly, his death could not be regarded as premature, for he had arrived at the ripe age
of three score and ten, and had left a public record
of a worthy life. Throughout the many temptations
of public life, which especially beset the statesman
and official characters on this continent, he had
walked with a firm step, keeping his eye fixed on
first principles, and never deviating into the tor-
tuous paths of expediency or injustice, as against
a certain class of helpless men. His career had been
a long one, and, as far as the speaker remembered,
the name of Giddings had always been familiar to

...his own act, vindicate" his position on our soil. The
whole affair moves on like the acts of a tragedy.
His first appearance is at a " Democratic" District
Convention, where he is chosen a delegate to Chicago. The next day, a State Convention in Illinois
pass resolutions in his honor, and pledge the Democracy for his defence. They array themselves for
a conflict with the Government, and seek thus to ex-
cite serious troubles in the Northwest for effect in
the Presidential campaign.

The instant this conspiracy reaches the open violation of the laws, it should, and doubtless will be
crushed by the strong arm. But the authorities
should be in no haste to fall into the snare set for
them. Vallandigham is a creature of no great account. So long as he is " the only man of the party
who is a victim to arbitrary power," he may well be
left to run at large. He is doing no harm by recov-
ing his testimony to this effect : " For more than one
year, no public man has been arrested or newspaper
suppressed within the State for an expression of
opinion, while hundreds in public assemblages and
through the press, with language and violence
which I never indulged, have criticised and condemned the acts and policy of the Administration,
denounced the war, and maintained even the pro-
priety of recognizing the Southern Confederacy.
His sentence of close custody may be wisely held in
suspense, while he is put upon his good behavior.
He is small game, not worth the commotion which
his re-arrest would occasion. It will be well enough
to keep an eye upon him, and upon those into whose
counsels he comes. Overt acts of treason, any open
manifestation of conspiracy against the Government
should be met by preparations ample to thwart and
punish them. But it would be worse than folly,
and, to lift Vallandigham to the rank of
... of a serious outbreak. The wise course of
Government will be, to let him severely alone
... he shall venture to play the traitor still fur...
him. In that case, the laws provide a punishment
...him.

... he shall be left thus to himself, he can make
... factitious capital, and will prove a sharp a...
... ing thorn in the side of the Democracy. He
... ments he is frank enough to express. The ...
... synonym for all that is odious in political pa...
to the loyal people. He will be at Chicago, ...
...to the Convention. The candidate...

The Liberator *reflected the strong
anti-slavery opinions of its publisher,
William Lloyd Garrison. Founded in
1831, the highly controversial paper
continued to be published until 1865,
when the 13th Amendment to the
Constitution ended slavery.*

cases it was a crime even to receive anti-slavery literature. In Georgia, under an 1835 law, the editor of a newspaper that opposed slavery could be punished by death.

In the North, in contrast, dozens of abolitionist newspapers sprang up to oppose slavery. But they often ran afoul of public opinion, if not the law. One of the best-known abolitionists, William Lloyd Garrison, who published the anti-slavery paper *The Liberator* in Boston, was dragged through the streets by an angry mob. Like others of the time, Garrison framed his arguments in strong terms. He believed that moral law outweighed civil law, and his paper carried such statements as, "The existing Constitution of the United States is a convenant with death and an agreement with hell."[5] To illustrate the point, he once burned a copy of the document in public.

Another abolitionist editor, Elijah Lovejoy, was killed for his statements. In the 1830s, Lovejoy published *The Observer* in St. Louis, Missouri, then a rough-and-tumble border town where opinion on slavery was mixed. Lovejoy opposed not only slavery but Irish immigration and Roman Catholicism as well, and the fact that St. Louis had a large and growing Irish population may have had as much to do with his unpopularity there as did the slavery issue. In any case, after a mob attacked his office and dumped part of his press into the Mississippi River, Lovejoy moved his paper across the river to Alton, Illinois. But his fiery words soon stirred up opposition there, too. Angry mobs destroyed his press twice; finally, in November 1837, Lovejoy was shot dead while trying to defend a third press from the same fate.

Lovejoy's story underscores an important point: In a democratic society, it is *unpopular* opinion—not the view of the majority—that is in danger of suppression. That point would be made clear again in the years to come.

Unpopular Speech. The Civil War brought new restrictions on freedom of expression, in the name of national security (discussed in Chapter 5). Those restrictions ended with the war. But the years after the war saw great social change. The late 1800s and early 1900s brought waves of immigrants to the United States, many of whom found work in factories and industries that boomed after the war. At the same time, new social ideas began to emerge. Workers began to form labor unions and strike to win higher wages and better working conditions. Radical political ideas were put forward—anarchism (the belief that all government should be abolished) and socialism (a system under which property and industries are controlled collectively or by the state). To many people in the United States, the immigrants, the labor unions, and the new ideas posed a threat to the American way of life.

No group raised more alarm than the Industrial Workers of the World (IWW). The Wobblies, as members of this group were called, included people from various walks of life—construction workers, migrant farm laborers, and others—as well as political radicals who called for the establishment of a socialist state. As the Wobblies' numbers grew, mostly in the South and West, local government leaders took steps to silence them by denying them the right to speak and assemble. Los Angeles, for example, made it illegal "to discuss, expound, advocate or oppose the principles or creed of any political party, partisan body, or organization, or religious denomination or sect, or the doctrines of any economic or social system in any public speech, lecture, or discourse, made or delivered in any public park in the City of Los Angeles."[6]

The Wobblies responded by staging "free speech fights" in more than two dozen cities, defying the laws by continuing to speak in public. They were arrested for such infractions as reading the Declaration of Inde-

Members of the Industrial Workers
of America, known as Wobblies, hoped
to lead a general strike to overthrow
the capitalist system. Their right to
stage demonstrations, such as the
one shown here in 1914 in New York
City, was curtailed by local government
leaders, who disagreed with their
unpopular philosophy.

pendence in public. In some cases, they were roughed up by the police or beaten by vigilantes, who also forced them to kiss the American flag. Hauled into court, they lost some of their cases but won others.

By 1916, the Wobblies' free speech fights had begun to draw support from moderate, middle-class Americans who were more alarmed by government attacks on freedom of expression than by the labor group's radical politics. But in 1917, the United States entered World War I, and fears about national security mounted. States passed laws prohibiting "seditious" speech and writing, and Congress passed the Espionage Act of 1917. This law, which made it illegal to promote disloyalty in the armed forces or obstruct recruitments, was expanded by the Sedition Act of 1918, which made it a crime to write or publish "any disloyal, profane, scurrilous or abusive language about the form of government of the United States or the Constitution, military or naval forces, flag, or the uniform," or to use language that would bring them "into contempt, scorn . . . or disrepute."[7]

At about the same time, the Russian revolution fanned a huge "Red scare"—a wave of apprehension over communist and socialist ideas. Thus, under the strict new laws, most of the IWW leaders were promptly arrested. So were leaders of the Socialist party. And so were less well-known people, such as Rose Pastor Stokes, who wrote in a letter to the editor of the *Kansas City Star*: "No government which is for the profiteers can also be for the people, and I am for the people, while the government is for the profiteers." She received a ten-year prison term, but the verdict was later reversed.[8]

The Supreme Court and Political Speech. The World War I laws prompted the first of what would be a series of Supreme Court decisions on freedom of expression. These decisions, made in cases appealed from lower courts, eventually established a body of "case law" through which the First Amendment rights of free speech were defined and interpreted.

The Court's role began after Charles Schenck, the general secretary of the Socialist party, was arrested in 1917 for urging resistance to the military draft. Specifically, Schenck and other Socialist party members had mailed about 15,000 leaflets to potential draftees, telling them that it was their right and duty to resist. He was convicted, and the Supreme Court upheld the conviction unanimously in 1919. But the Court's opinion, written by Justice Oliver Wendell Holmes, stressed the wartime circumstances of Schenck's offense: "When a nation is at war many things that might be said in time of peace are such a hindrance to its effort that their utterance will not be endured." The central question in any limit on expression, Holmes wrote, was whether that expression would create a "clear and present danger." And danger depended on circumstances—"The most stringent protection of free speech would not protect a man in falsely shouting fire in a crowded theatre and causing a panic."[9]

Just eight months later, Holmes found himself opposing the majority of the Court in another free-speech case. This case involved an anarchist, Jacob Abrams, who received a twenty-year prison term for dumping leaflets out tenement windows in New York City. The leaflets criticized the government for sending troops into Russia, called President Woodrow Wilson a coward, and urged munitions workers to strike and to "spit in the face [of] the false, hypocritic, military propaganda which has fooled you so relentlessly."[10] The Supreme Court upheld Abrams's conviction, citing *Schenck*. But two justices, Holmes and Louis D. Brandeis, dissented, holding that the government had failed to show that Abrams's "silly"

(39)

leaflets posed any real threat to the U.S. war effort. Echoing Milton, Holmes wrote: "The best test of truth is the power of thought to get itself accepted in the competition of the market. . . . That at any rate is the theory of our Constitution." To ensure that competition, he said, "We should be eternally vigilant against attempts to check the expression of ideas we loathe."[11]

Holmes and Brandeis dissented again in 1925, when the Court upheld the conviction of Benjamin Gitlow. Gitlow, a Socialist, had published pamphlets that called for revolution; he was convicted under a New York state law that made it a crime to advocate the overthrow of government. The United States was no longer at war, and the Court did not find that Gitlow's work posed any immediate danger. Instead, the majority held that his words might do harm at some unspecified future time—they produced a "bad tendency."

Gitlow's case did lead to one advance in freedom of expression, however. Until that time, the Court had ruled only in speech cases that involved the federal government—but this case involved a state law. Even as it upheld Gitlow's conviction, the Court ruled for the first time that the First Amendment's protections applied to state as well as federal government. It based this ruling on the Fourteenth Amendment, passed after the Civil War, which states in part that "no state shall make or enforce any law which shall abridge the privileges or immunities of citizens of the United States."

Strengthening Freedom of Expression. That principle was applied again in a landmark press freedom case, *Near v. Minnesota,* in 1931. Jay M. Near was a journalist in Minneapolis, Minnesota, with a reputation for writing gossipy exposés. In 1927 his weekly, the *Saturday Press,* ran a series of articles linking local officials to illegal gambling operations, criticizing the officials in vehement, often anti-Semitic terms. Citing a state law that outlawed as a public nuisance any obscene or "malicious, scandalous and defamatory newspaper," a county prosecutor obtained an injunction against Near—a court order forbidding publication.[12] The injunction was so broad that it banned past as well as future issues of the *Saturday Press,* and it barred Near from publishing any other paper that attacked public officials.

When Near's case reached the Supreme Court three and a half years later, the majority ruled in his favor. Minnesota's "gag" law, the Court held, violated the First Amendment by imposing prior restraint—that is, by blocking expression before it took place. Chief Justice Charles E. Hughes took up the idea of "clear and present danger" and, citing Holmes's opinion in *Schenck,* wrote that few situations called for such censorship: disclosing troop movements in wartime, obstructing recruiting efforts, inciting acts of violence or the overthrow of government by force. None of these applied in *Near.* Nor did it matter if Near's allegations were true or false— "Some degree of abuse is inseparable from the proper use of everything, and in no instance is this more true than in that of the press," Hughes wrote.[13] However, if they were false, Near could be held accountable *after* publication.

The Court again broadened its stand on freedom of expression five years later, in a case that had begun in Oregon in 1934. The country then was in the grip of the Great Depression; in Portland, Oregon, longshoremen were on strike. The strike sparked violence—longshoremen clashed with police and with vigilante groups. In the midst of this, Dirk DeJonge, a leader in the Oregon Communist party, held a rally to protest police brutality. Midway through the meeting, the police moved in and arrested DeJonge and the other speakers. They were charged under a state law that outlawed any doctrine that advocated "crime, physical violence, arson, destruction of property, sabotage, or other unlawful acts as means of accomplishing or effecting industrial or political ends." It was against the law to join an organization that advocated such acts, or even to assemble with people who did.[14] Neither DeJonge nor the other speakers had preached such a doctrine at the meeting; but they were convicted because the meeting was held under the auspices of the Communist party, which had been known to advocate sabotage. Tried separately, DeJonge received the harshest sentence—a seven-year prison term. In December 1936, the Supreme Court heard his appeal.

The Court ruled unanimously in his favor, declaring that he had a right to discuss the public issues of the day. Chief Justice Hughes wrote that the importance of safeguarding public institutions from violent overthrow made it imperative to preserve, not limit, freedom of expression and freedom of assembly—only through those freedoms could the will of the people be heard and change made peacefully.

In the space of less than twenty years, the Supreme Court had moved from a stand that permitted government great leeway in restricting speech to one that gave great protection to individuals, no matter how unpopular their opinions. But the stand was by no means absolute; even in *DeJonge,* the Court alluded to "permissible" limits on expression.

Defining those limits proved to be a problem, and unpopular opinions would come under attack again. In the 1940s, the country was swept by another "Red scare." Congress passed the Smith Act, which (among other provisions) made it a federal offense to advocate the overthrow of government by force, or to belong to a group or publish, edit, distribute, or display printed matter that did. In 1948, eleven Communists were convicted under the law, and the Supreme Court upheld their convictions. But in 1957 the Court threw out the convictions of fourteen other Communists convicted under the same law. This time the Court drew a fine and somewhat hazy line between advocating action (not permissible) and advocating ideas (permissible, even when the ideas might include the theoretical use of violence). The ruling made it extremely difficult to convict anyone under the Smith Act, and government prosecutions ended.

"The Thought We Hate." In 1978 the protection offered by the First Amendment was tested to the limit in one of the most famous free-speech cases of recent times. The case began when the National Socialist Party of America, a Chicago offshoot of the American Nazi party, requested permission to march in Skokie, Illinois. This idea was particularly repugnant to Skokie; not only were more than half of the residents Jewish, but at least five thousand were survivors of the Holocaust and remembered all too well the atrocities inflicted by the German Nazi party on Jews during World War II. Skokie officials replied that the American Nazis would have to post a $350,000 insurance bond if they wanted to march. The Nazis in turn announced that they would hold a peaceful protest rally in front of Skokie's Village Hall, displaying the party symbol of the swastika and demanding "free speech for white people."[15]

The town's attorney promptly obtained a court injunction to block the demonstration, and the village council passed a pair of ordinances that, besides requiring the insurance bond, gave the government the right to censor public gatherings and bar rallies by groups that wore military-style uniforms or promoted hatred on racial, ethnic, national, or religious grounds. A third ordinance made it a crime to distribute printed material that promoted hatred on those grounds.

The Nazis brought two lawsuits, one to lift the injunction and the other to overturn the village ordinances, and for over a year the cases wound through half a dozen courts. Skokie's attorneys did not see the town's action as a violation of the First Amendment. To them, "the symbol of the swastika was not an expression of protected free speech. It amounted to an assault just as much as a physical assault."[16] Some 600,000 Americans agreed and signed petitions supporting the village. Others felt even more strongly; some of the lawyers who argued the Nazis' case in court received anonymous death threats.

The Skokie case troubled many Americans deeply. In Europe, Nazi doctrines had led to the deaths of millions in concentration camps and to a devastating war that had taken the lives of millions more. To hear these same doctrines freely advocated on American streets was abhorrent. Yet to ban them raised other troubling questions. If these doctrines were too repugnant to permit, then others might be banned as well, whenever public outrage so demanded. In fact, if public opinion ruled, any unpopular view might be suppressed—as anti-slavery opinions were in the South before the Civil War.

Ultimately, the Illinois Supreme Court decided in the Nazis' favor and lifted the ban on the march; a federal district court then overturned the village ordinances. The federal judge in the case cited words written by Justice Holmes in an earlier case: "If there is any principle of the Constitution that more imperatively calls for attachment than any other it is the principle of free thought— not free thought for those who agree with us but freedom for the thought we hate." Freedom of thought, the federal

*What appears to be a scene from Nazi
Germany is actually a photo of a
neo-Nazi group marching in Chicago
in 1978. Although the law upheld the
right of the group to demonstrate,
their fellow citizens responded with a
barrage of eggs, sticks, firecrackers,
and beer cans—thus, the shields.*

court judge added, carries with it "the freedom to speak and to publicly assemble to express one's thoughts."[17]

The U.S. Supreme Court declined to hear Skokie's appeal, allowing the Illinois ruling to stand. The Nazis marched—but in the end, they did it in Chicago, where they were vastly outnumbered by counterdemonstrators.

4

"Fighting Words" and "Speech Plus"

In Skokie, town officials banned display of the swastika and the wearing of military-style uniforms, arguing that the sight of swastikas and Nazi uniforms might provoke violence. That argument touched on two gray areas of the First Amendment: whether speech can be limited if it may lead to public disturbance or violence, and the line between speech and action. With broad protection for unpopular opinions firmly established by the series of cases from *Schenck* to Skokie, disagreement over the meaning of the amendment has increasingly focused on questions such as these—because restrictions on when, where, and how opinions are expressed can be used to suppress unpopular ideas.

Fighting Words. The Skokie case was not the first to raise these issues. Seven years earlier, as protests against the Vietnam War were sweeping the country, the U.S. Supreme Court addressed them in the case of Paul Robert Cohen. Cohen, a young Californian who opposed both the war and military conscription, took to wearing a jacket emblazoned with the words "F___ THE DRAFT." When he wore the jacket in a hallway of the Los Angeles County Courthouse, he was arrested and later convicted under a California law that made it a crime to "maliciously and willfully disturb the peace . . . by . . . offensive conduct."[1]

State prosecutors cited the offensive language on the jacket and argued that it was likely to provoke violence from onlookers. In this, they looked back to earlier court decisions that had excluded what became known as "fighting words" from First Amendment protection. In 1942, for example, the Supreme Court had upheld the conviction of a New Hampshire man who had been arrested after telling a police officer, "You are a goddamned racketeer . . . a damned fascist," because his words were judged likely to provoke an immediate violent reaction.[2]

But the Court had also made it clear that restrictions on "fighting words" could not be broadly applied. In 1949, it had overturned the conviction of a Chicago priest who was arrested for disturbing the peace after he gave an inflammatory, racist speech. The priest, Father Arthur W. Terminiello, had already been suspended by the Roman Catholic Church for his vitriolic attacks on Jews, blacks, and other groups; and fights did in fact break out between his supporters and opponents after his speech. But by a narrow vote of 5–4, the Court found that "a function of free speech under our system of government is to invite dispute." Delivering a speech was a form of expression that could not be restricted unless it was "likely to produce a clear and present danger of a serious substantive evil that rises far above public inconvenience, annoyance, or unrest."[3]

In Paul Robert Cohen's case, however, the California courts held that *conduct,* not simply speech, was at issue: Cohen's act of wearing a jacket with a four-letter word was likely to provoke others to violence; thus, he was guilty of disturbing the peace. But the Supreme Court disagreed. The crux of the case was the message the jacket bore, and that, the Court said, was a matter of *communication.* Writing for the majority, Justice John Marshall Harlan gave three reasons for preventing states from "punishing public utterance . . . to maintain what they regard as a suitable level of [public] discourse."[4]

First was the concept of the marketplace of ideas— "verbal tumult, discord, and even offensive utterance" are "necessary side effects of the broader enduring values which the process of open debate allows us to achieve," Harlan said. Second, the state's objection to the expletive on Cohen's jacket was arbitrary. "One man's vulgarity is another man's lyric," Harlan wrote; if governments were allowed to regulate language, they "might soon seize upon the censorship of particular words as a convenient guise for banning the expression of unpopular views." Third, Harlan noted that speakers commonly choose vulgarities to convey powerful emotions that "may often be the more important element of the overall message." In other words, First Amendment protection is not limited to dry, reasoned arguments—it extends to passionate expressions of opinion as well.

In later cases, the Court threw out on various grounds convictions for such direct insults as "white son of a bitch, I'll kill you," and "m____ f____ fascist pig cop," making the doctrine of "fighting words" virtually a dead issue.[5] Strong dissenting opinions in these cases (and in *Terminiello* and *Cohen*) left open the possibility that the doctrine might be revived. (The Court has often cited dissents when it departs from past rulings.) But the gist of these rulings was that government cannot pick and choose the vocabulary of public debate any more than it can control the opinions that are expressed, and that a hostile audience is not a reason to suppress an idea.

Speech Plus. What about purely symbolic expressions of opinion—expressions that, like the display of a swastika, contain no words at all? Again, the Skokie case was not the first to raise the issue—nor would it be the last. When Gregory Lee Johnson set a match to the U.S. flag in 1984, few people would have argued that his right to criticize the government was not protected by the Constitution. But the public outcry that arose showed that many were unwilling to give that same protection to a symbolic act such as flag burning.

Symbolic expression, or "speech plus" as it is sometimes called, has grown in importance in recent years—partly, perhaps, because it gets media attention. Television (the main source of news for most people) is a visual medium. If you give a twenty-minute speech on the steps of city hall, the evening news may not even cover it. But a dramatic act—holding a sit-in, hanging the mayor in effigy, burning the flag—makes good videotape. Not only is it sure to be aired, but it can make a point quickly and in an emotional way that words rarely can.

Flag burning in particular seems to set off strong emotions—but views on this have changed over the years. For almost the first century of the country's existence, most Americans would have scoffed at the idea of regulating the use (or abuse) of the flag. Americans were not unpatriotic, but the flag itself was not held in any special reverence—for years the design wasn't even standardized. That changed in the 1890s, when concern about immigration and labor unrest made many people feel that American values were threatened. In addition, the flag was an issue in the presidential election campaign of 1896, when it was displayed prominently at rallies for the candidates William McKinley and William Jennings Bryan. Supporters of one candidate often ripped down the flags of the other's—and, in some cases, pelted them with rotten eggs or blasted them with shotguns—as if only their candidate had a right to display the banner.

The next year, a group called the American Flag Association was formed to promote legal protection for the flag, and Pennsylvania became the first state to make it a crime to damage or destroy the flag. Other states followed quickly. The first national flag law came in 1942, when Congress adopted a resolution providing guidelines for the correct use of the flag. Still, there were no penalties for not following the guidelines. But attitudes hardened during the Vietnam War, when flag burning and other symbolic acts (such as flying the flag upside down) became a form of antiwar protest. In 1968, Congress imposed criminal penalties on anyone who "knowingly casts contempt upon any flag of the United States by publicly mutilating, defacing, defiling, burning or trampling on it."[6] States also began to vigorously enforce their flag statutes.

The result was a series of court cases. One was that of Valerie Goguen, a young man who was arrested in Leominster, Massachusetts, for wearing jeans that were patched on the seat with a small American flag. Goguen did not claim to be protesting anything (he said his jeans needed a patch), but when his case reached the U.S. Supreme Court in 1974 (as *Smith, Sheriff* v. *Goguen*), the justices struck down the Massachusetts flag law that had led to his arrest. For the majority of the justices, the main reason was that the law was too vague—it made it a crime to treat the flag "contemptuously" and left it to government officials to decide what contemptuous treatment might be. That made it too difficult for people to know when they might be breaking the law. Only one justice, Byron White, found that the law violated the First

Amendment because it prevented the symbolic expression of opinions about the flag.

In another 1974 case, a university student was arrested after he attached a peace symbol to a flag and hung it upside down from the window of his apartment. He ran afoul of a Washington state law that made it a crime to "place . . . any . . . design . . . upon any flag" of the United States.[7] The state courts ruled that government had a legitimate interest in preserving the flag as a symbol of the country, but the Supreme Court reversed that ruling 5–4. However, the justices did not deny that government might have an interest in preserving the flag as a symbol—they found only that the protest in question hadn't seriously threatened the flag's symbolic value.

In fact, the Court had earlier upheld bans on symbolic acts that it found threatened government interests. Besides flags, antiwar protesters of the Vietnam War era burned draft cards—cards issued by the Selective Service administration that, by law, were to be carried by young men of draft age. In a 1968 case (*United States v. O'Brien*), the Court had found that even if burning a draft card was a form of expression, the government's interest in requiring men to carry the card was strong enough to outweigh any First Amendment right.

The upshot of all these cases was that "speech plus" remained a somewhat vague concept, and bans on flag desecration remained on the books in forty-eight states and in the federal code. But when the issue of flag burning emerged again a decade later in *Texas v. Johnson*, the Supreme Court's majority clearly placed the act under the protection of the First Amendment.

The state based its case on two arguments—that Johnson's act disturbed the peace and that the state had an interest in preserving the symbolic value of the flag. The Court rejected the first, noting that no disturbance

Gregory Johnson, whose conviction for torching a U.S. flag was overturned by the Supreme Court, poses with a charred flag.

broke out when the flag was burned. And on the question of the flag's symbolic value, the majority opinion said that government had no right to decree that a symbol such as the flag could be used to present only one view. Johnson had burned the flag to express dissatisfaction with the state of politics in the country; that use of the symbol, the Court said, was fully protected under the First Amendment.

Four justices dissented. Several, including Chief Justice William H. Rehnquist, would have granted the flag special protected status; and the fact that many people agreed was made clear by the public outcry that greeted the ruling. With state and federal flag laws in effect ruled unconstitutional by the *Johnson* decision, Congress answered the outcry by passing a new antidesecration law. That law was immediately challenged, and in 1990 the Supreme Court struck it down as well (*United States* v. *Eichman*).

The only way to forbid flag burning, it appeared, would be to amend the Constitution to give the flag special status as a symbol of the nation. Such an amendment was introduced in Congress in 1990, with the strong support of President George Bush. But by the time Congress voted on the measure, passions had cooled. The attempt to change the Constitution to limit the protection of the First Amendment was unprecedented, and many lawmakers worried that it might open the door for other restrictions on freedom of expression. As time went on, polls showed that many citizens were concerned as well—public opinion was swinging against the amendment. When the vote finally came, the amendment failed to get the two-thirds majority it needed.

Free Speech and Hate Crimes. The Supreme Court's ruling in *Johnson* and similar cases helped clarify the "speech plus" issue. In the Court's reasoning, government can't forbid an action simply because the action expresses an offensive opinion. But acts that endanger people or damage property can be prohibited. And generally, actions that interfere with some legitimate interest are not protected—for example, opponents of abortion may demonstrate outside abortion clinics, but if they block a clinic's door and prevent patients from entering, the demonstrators are likely to be arrested. The key in these cases is that the actions themselves—not the messages they are designed to convey—create the problem.

But questions about just which actions can be restricted remain. In 1991, those questions were at the heart of a controversy over laws against "hate crimes"—crimes motivated by bias against racial, religious, or ethnic groups or against women. All but four states had adopted such laws in the 1980s. Most of the laws simply assigned stiffer penalties when crimes such as assault were motivated by bias. But in a few cases, the laws went further and made certain *expressions* of bias a crime.

The issue reached the Supreme Court in 1991 through a case that originated in St. Paul, Minnesota. There, in June 1990, two teenagers burned a cross on the lawn of the sole black family in Mounds Park, a white, working-class neighborhood. They were arrested under a St. Paul ordinance that made it a misdemeanor to place "on public or private property a symbol, object, appellation, characterization or graffiti, including but not limited to a burning cross or Nazi swastika, which one knows or has reasonable grounds to know arouses anger, alarm or resentment in others on the basis of race, color, religion or gender."[8] One of the two teenagers pleaded guilty and served thirty days in jail; the other, Robert A. Viktora, challenged the ordinance as unconstitutional.

Like the Skokie case more than a decade earlier, this

The Court must deal with the legality of the racially motivated threat symbolized by the burning cross versus the freedom of individuals to express their views via words or symbols.

case raised issues that many people found deeply troubling. Cross burning has long been associated with groups such as the Ku Klux Klan and with racially motivated mob violence and lynching. To Russ and Laura Jones, on whose lawn the cross had appeared, it was a clear threat—"A burning cross is a way of saying, 'We're going to get you,'" Laura Jones told an interviewer.[9] The Minnesota Supreme Court agreed, holding that a burning cross "is itself an unmistakable symbol of violence and hatred based on virulent notions of racial supremacy."[10] As such, the act of burning a cross could be seen as an incitement to violence.

Yet the burning cross was also an expression of opinion, and many people who opposed the act also questioned the law that banned it. "The First Amendment is almost always tested with speech that is profoundly divisive or painful," said Lawrence Tribe, a professor of constitutional law at Harvard University. "But if you start making exceptions, and suppressing speech that is hurtful, those exceptions will swallow free speech."[11]

The Supreme Court's ruling came in June 1992. All nine justices agreed that the St. Paul ordinance was unconstitutional, but they differed sharply on the reasons. Four justices argued that, while this law was too broad, governments might ban forms of hate speech that were likely to lead to violence. But five—the majority—held that the law violated the First Amendment because it restricted speech on the basis of content. (The majority included two newly appointed justices, David Souter and Clarence Thomas, who had replaced retired justices William Brennan and Thurgood Marshall.) In this view, virtually any hate-speech law that focused on the message, rather than the means of expression, would violate the Constitution.

5

The Press and National Security

In 1991, at the start of the Persian Gulf War, U.S. and allied troops massed in Saudi Arabia and began a drive to push Iraqi forces out of Kuwait. People in the United States and around the world saw military briefings, air-raid alerts— even scenes from Baghdad, Iraq—reported on the spot via television satellite links. The heavy news coverage gave most viewers the impression that they were witnesses to the war, receiving a full and complete picture. Yet in fact, news coverage was perhaps more restricted in this war than in any other U.S. conflict.

Most of the more than one thousand reporters who were on the scene never got closer to the action than Riyadh or Dhahran, Saudi Arabia, towns far from the front. Only about one hundred were assigned to press pools that were allowed to talk to the half million U.S. troops in the region, and that number included camera operators, technicians, and others who were not actually reporters. They traveled with and conducted their interviews in the presence of military escorts; some who tried to work independently were detained by the authorities.

Cartoonist Tom Gibb pokes fun at the press briefings offered by General Schwarzkopf during the Persian Gulf War.

In addition, all reports were screened by the military before release.

The military advanced several reasons for the restrictions—the difficulty of desert transportation, the safety of reporters, and above all the need to keep sensitive military information out of the hands of the enemy. But, intended or not, the result was that the picture of the war that Americans saw on their television screens was the picture that the military wanted them to see.

The tight control of information raised two important questions. First, how broad is government's right to restrict speech in the name of national security? And second, if the First Amendment protects expression mainly to ensure open, democratic government, does that mean that there is a public "right to know"? In other words, does the Constitution require government to make information public, so that voters can make informed decisions?

From the time of the Alien and Sedition Acts, national security has been the reason most often cited when government attempts to restrict speech or withhold information. The press, which is in the business of providing information, has run up against this argument in times of peace as well as times of war.

Censorship in Wartime. Wartime censorship first emerged during the Civil War, when hundreds of reporters from North and South alike fanned out to cover the conflict. By and large, their actions were not restricted (although General William Tecumseh Sherman, for one, regarded reporters as "spies" and would not allow them to travel with his troops). But President Abraham Lincoln did take broad powers in the name of national security. He suspended habeas corpus (the right of anyone taken into custody to receive a prompt court hearing) and censored the mails to keep anti-Union literature from circulating. Military commanders could silence the expression of ideas and information they thought might harm the war effort, and they fined or briefly suspended several newspapers that opposed the government.

Censorship ended with the war. But the reasoning behind it—that government could suspend civil liberties to protect the country from a threat to national security—reemerged during World War I, in the 1917 Espionage Act and the 1918 Sedition Act. While these laws were used to silence "disloyal" opinions in the United States, reporters still had great freedom to cover the war. In most areas, they could travel without restriction and visit the front lines without a military escort. But all reports passed through military censors who could remove unauthorized information about troop movements, casualties, and the like.

A similar system operated during World War II. In addition, the government's wartime Office of Censorship issued guidelines for reporters, telling them how to handle news of troops, planes, ships, war production, and even weather. Most reporters supported the war effort and bent over backward to comply, but they chafed under some of the restrictions. For example, details of the damage done in the Japanese attack on Pearl Harbor were withheld by the Navy on the ground that the Japanese should not have the information. Reporters complained that the Navy was also hiding evidence of its own unpreparedness and inefficiency.[1]

Cold War Restrictions. The years after World War II saw growing friction between the press and government over national security. In 1951, as Cold War tensions grew, President Harry S. Truman asserted that "newspapers and slick magazines" had revealed ninety-five percent of U.S.

military secrets.[2] He called on all branches of government to classify information top secret, secret, confidential, or restricted, as had been done by the military.

The results were sometimes bizarre. On the grounds of national security, a recipe for cherry upside-down cake was classified confidential by the Department of Agriculture. The Danbury, Connecticut, *News-Times* received an Army press release marked "confidential" about a corporal's promotion to sergeant. And a team of security officers was sent to San Francisco to investigate a "top secret" leak after a newspaper printed a story, taken from public records in city hall, about a proposal to use ten acres of city land to train dogs for the military.[3]

While later presidents may have advocated less secrecy, all on occasion affirmed that government had the power to restrict information in the national interest. In 1961, after the U.S. Central Intelligence Agency (CIA) sponsored a secret invasion of Cuba at the Bay of Pigs, President John F. Kennedy placed some of the blame for the invasion's failure on newspaper reports that appeared beforehand. "Every newspaper now asks itself, with respect to every story, 'Is it news?' All I suggest is that you add the question, 'Is it in the national interest?'" he admonished publishers.[4] Large newspapers such as the *Washington Post* and *The New York Times* protested that they had actually withheld information about the invasion. (In fact, Kennedy was reported to have told the *Times* managing editor privately that if the paper had printed more about the operation, it "would have saved us from a colossal mistake."[5]) But *The Nation,* a small-circulation magazine that had been among the first to hint at the invasion plan, countered in an editorial:

We are said to be an open society, in which the press reports the news and is free to praise, criticize or condemn. In this open society, by this mechanism, the government is to be responsible to public opinion. Actually public opinion has ceased to function, for the government proceeded in secrecy, most of the press abetted it, and the public was faced with a fait accompli and invited to rally around the flag.[6]

As foreign policy, the Bay of Pigs invasion was a fiasco. It also soured relations between the press and government, increasing mistrust on both sides. That mistrust became full-blown within the decade, during the Vietnam War.

The Press in Vietnam. The Vietnam War received what may have been the most thorough news coverage of any war in history. In addition, television added a new dimension, bringing the sights and sounds of war directly into homes throughout the United States. The conflict, in which the United States backed South Vietnam against Communist guerrillas and the Communist government of North Vietnam, split opinion in the United States—some people saw it as an essential part of the global struggle against Communism, while others saw it as an unwarranted intervention in a civil war.

Opinion was no less divided in the press. Increasingly, however, correspondents came to doubt the official version of events—less because the government put out false reports than because it released only good news and because it tended to label as victories engagements that were in fact inconclusive (as are many actions in a guerrilla war). The steady message from the government was that the United States and South Vietnam were winning the war. Reporters, who once again had great freedom of movement, often saw a different view: corrupt South Vietnamese officials, a South Vietnamese army that was ill prepared and sometimes refused to fight, botched military actions that took a heavy toll in civilian lives, and occasional atrocities.

Press reports had their greatest impact in 1968, when the Vietnamese Communists staged a massive offensive in late January, during the Tet holiday period. Communist forces, which until then had fought mostly in the countryside, took the battle to cities such as Hue and Saigon, where they put the U.S. embassy under siege. They were beaten back with heavy losses; in fact, the Tet offensive was a serious defeat for the Communists. But many reporters were taken aback by the sudden and widespread nature of the offensive. How could victory be around the corner, as government reports suggested, if the Communists could seemingly attack anywhere at any time? News coverage reflected this view and helped tip public opinion against the war.[7]

Besides, government attempts to manage the news often backfired. In 1969, President Richard Nixon ordered a "secret" bombing campaign in Cambodia, where the Vietcong had bases. When a report of the bombing appeared in *The New York Times,* he condemned the story as a violation of national security. But as Benjamin Bradlee, executive editor of the *Washington Post,* noted:

> *The Cambodians certainly knew they were being bombed. . . . If the Cambodians knew, the Vietcong knew. And if the Vietcong knew, their Soviet allies knew immediately. So what was all that about? Well, the American people didn't know, and in fact they had been told we would not bomb Cambodia . . . national security was used to cover up a national embarrassment.*[8]

Incidents such as this served to deepen mistrust between the government and the press—and, ultimately, the public.

The Pentagon Papers. The tension between government and the press formed the backdrop for a court battle in which the government attempted to block publication of what it called sensitive information about the war. In 1971, *The New York Times* obtained a forty-seven-volume top-secret Pentagon study that traced the historical and political roots of U.S. involvement in Vietnam. When the newspaper began a series of stories based on the study, the Nixon administration immediately obtained a court order barring further publication. Meanwhile, the *Washington Post* also began to publish stories based on the study, known as the Pentagon Papers. But in Washington, a federal court refused the government's request to block publication.

Both cases were appealed to the Supreme Court, which ruled 6-3 against the government, citing the protection against prior restraint that had been affirmed in *Near* v. *Minnesota* and other cases. The Court said that any government attempt at prior restraint bears a "heavy presumption against its constitutional validity" and that government "thus carries a heavy burden of showing justification" for the restraint. Here, the Court said, the government failed to show that publishing the Pentagon Papers material would create a clear and present danger to U.S. troops.[9]

The verdict was hailed as a victory for freedom of expression, but it was no landmark. For one thing, the nine justices issued nine separate opinions, reflecting a wide spectrum of views. At one end were Justices Douglas and Black, who held that any government attempt to suppress speech was unconstitutional. In Black's words: "The press was protected by the First Amendment

A Federal judge granted the government a temporary order restraining The New York Times *from publishing the last two installments of a Pentagon study of the Vietnam War. Shown here are the first three installments published before the order, which was later overturned by the Supreme Court.*

so that it could bare the secrets of government and inform the people."[10] Other justices saw the case more narrowly—some based the decision on the fact that Congress had not specifically authorized court orders as a means of withholding information. And the three dissenting opinions held that publication might have been delayed much longer, while the government outlined in depth its need to withhold the study.

Watergate and After. That government officials are willing to use "national security" to cover their own errors or misdeeds was made plain a few years later during the Watergate scandal. In this incident, the White House authorized a burglary of Democratic party headquarters at the Watergate apartment complex in Washington, D.C., and then orchestrated an elaborate cover-up of its involvement. Tapes of White House conversations ultimately confirmed President Nixon's role in the events and forced his resignation. But throughout most of the investigation, Nixon repeatedly cited national security as a reason for not releasing the tapes or revealing the truth about the incident.

Watergate led to a movement for greater openness in government. Under a strengthened federal Freedom of Information Act, the public learned about efforts by the CIA to assassinate foreign leaders and to develop ways to control the human mind. But there were also reactions against such openness, and in fact some disclosures did more harm than good. For example, a CIA agent was killed in Athens in 1975, less than a month after a newspaper published his name and revealed that he worked for the agency.

By the time President Ronald Reagan took office in 1981, the pendulum had swung in the opposite direction. The Reagan administration changed the rules on secrecy, directing officials to classify information unless there was reason to believe it would *not* harm national security—that is, to begin with a presumption of secrecy. The administration also aggressively pursued unauthorized "leaks" of information. One proposal would have required some 100,000 government employees to submit to censorship for the rest of their lives.

New restrictions were also placed on press coverage of military actions during the Reagan years. In 1983, the government blacked out news coverage completely during the invasion of Grenada, where U.S. troops were sent to overturn a leftist coup. After vehement press protests, a Pentagon panel recommended that "pools" of reporters be set up to cover the early hours of military actions, after which coverage should be as unrestricted as it was in the Vietnam War.

It was this pool system that was used during the 1991 Gulf War. However, the system limited press access during far more than the early hours of the war—it was used during the buildup that preceded the fighting and throughout the conflict.

Is There a "Right to Know"? The conflict between freedom of expression and national security remains unresolved. On the question of the government's right to censor material it considers sensitive, a long series of Supreme Court cases have clearly denied the right to block reports that do not pose a direct threat to national security. But "national security" is an elastic concept; often government itself decides what it is.

The second question—whether the public has a right to government information—is even harder to answer. Significantly, a majority of the Supreme Court has never held that there is any "right to know." But individual justices have argued that the right exists, unstated, in the

The single word "Reaganism,"
affixed to this Vic Cantone cartoon,
made a dramatic statement about the
restrictions imposed on the dissemination
of all types of information during the
Reagan presidency.

First Amendment's free-speech guarantee. Justice William O. Douglas, for one, quoted James Madison:

> *A popular government, without popular information, is but a prelude to a Farce or a Tragedy. . . . Knowledge will forever govern ignorance: And a people who mean to be their own Governors, must arm themselves with the power which knowledge gives.*[11]

The fact remains that the only source of information about government activities is often the government itself. Clearly, even the most democratic governments must hold some secrets, especially in the area of defense. But just as clearly, secrecy can undermine democracy by screening from public view the facts that voters need to know.

Damaging Speech

Although the debate over a public "right to know" continues, court orders suppressing speech or blocking publications are rare. But what about punishment *after the fact* for spreading information that does damage? The principle today is not very different from that outlined by the English jurist William Blackstone in the 1700s—individuals and the mass media alike may be held accountable for what they say or print. But there have been important changes in the way that principle is applied.

Libel. The most common method of bringing accountability to bear is through libel actions in the courts. Since Blackstone's time, the charge of "seditious libel"—a defamatory statement that undermines government authority—has gone by the boards. And the government has not prosecuted the media for making sensitive information public (although some government officials have suggested that this might be done, and individuals who released information to the public have been prosecuted). Instead, most libel suits are civil actions, brought by individuals who seek compensation for damage they claim has been done to their reputation.

Libel is a slippery concept, and the state laws that deal with it vary. Generally, they define libel as a published statement that defames a person—that is, holds someone up to public hatred, contempt, or ridicule or injures a person professionally. The legal definition of "published" isn't the usual one: A statement is published when it is seen by a third party. (Thus it's possible for a letter to be libelous.) When a defamatory statement is merely spoken, the wrong is called slander; but actions for slander are rare because the person bringing the charge must prove that he or she was injured in some specific way by the statement. Where libel is concerned, injury is usually assumed. (Broadcasting presents unique problems; generally, the laws of libel rather than slander apply to words spoken over the airwaves.)

As a rule, a person can't be sued for libel for publishing a true statement, no matter how defamatory. This was the defense that John Peter Zenger advanced in 1735; and it became widely recognized after 1804, when Alexander Hamilton used it to defend a Federalist editor in New York against a libel charge. (Hamilton actually lost the case, but he argued it so brilliantly that New York and other states soon passed laws allowing truth as a defense in libel actions.)* Other defenses have been established as well. A libel action can't generally be brought for a fair and accurate report of an official proceeding (a congressional debate, for example) or for a

---

* Libel would be Hamilton's undoing. While this case was being tried, a remark attributed to him by an Albany newspaper insulted Vice President Aaron Burr, who challenged him to a duel and shot him fatally on July 11, 1804.

clear statement of opinion about a matter of public interest (such as a film review or a newspaper editorial), as long as the opinion is based on fact.

But for nearly 175 years after the adoption of the First Amendment, libel was not considered a free-speech issue. False, defamatory statements were simply outside the protection of the amendment. Then, in 1964, a Supreme Court ruling brought a major change.

Libel and the First Amendment. The ruling grew out of the heated atmosphere of the civil rights movement of the 1950s and 1960s, when blacks were struggling to gain equal rights with whites. All too often, civil rights demonstrations met with brutality from the police; and such incidents provoked protests from supporters of the movement.

On March 29, 1960, *The New York Times* published a full-page ad, signed by sixty-four prominent people, that listed a series of complaints against the police in Montgomery, Alabama. Several of the statements in the ad were false. A city commissioner, L. B. Sullivan, filed suit, claiming that he had been defamed because it was his job to supervise the police. When the case went to trial, an Alabama jury awarded him $500,000 in damages. (Meanwhile, two other city commissioners and the governor of Alabama also filed suit, asking for a total of $2.5 million.)

The *Times* appealed, and the case reached the Supreme Court in 1964. The Court ruled unanimously that no damages should be awarded, and in doing so it broke new ground. The decision, written by Justice Brennan, held for the first time that libel "must be measured by standards that satisfy the First Amendment." Brennan wrote:

A full-page ad in The New York Times *on the brutality of the police department in Montgomery, Alabama, led to the landmark* Times v. Sullivan *case, which protected from libel laws individuals making critical remarks about "public officials."*

We consider this case against the background of a profound national commitment to the principle that debate on public issues should be uninhibited, robust, and wide-open, and that it may well include vehement, caustic, and sometimes unpleasantly sharp attacks on government and public officials.

Inevitably, Brennan held, such "uninhibited" debate would lead to some false statements—but if critics of government were required to guarantee the truth of every statement or face the threat of huge libel judgments, the result would be self-censorship. Instead, he wrote:

The constitutional guarantees require, we think, a federal rule that prohibits a public official from recovering damages for a defamatory falsehood relating to his official conduct unless he proves that the statement was made with "actual malice"—that is, with knowledge that it was false or with reckless disregard of whether it was false or not.[1]

The *Times* v. *Sullivan* ruling was a landmark because it extended First Amendment protection into a new area. But it left many questions, including the question of who should be considered a "public official" (consultants? maintenance workers?) and what, exactly, constituted "reckless disregard" of the truth. Later cases struggled with these points.

In 1967, for example, the Supreme Court ruled in a case involving Wally Butts, then athletic director at the University of Georgia. Butts had successfully sued the *Saturday Evening Post* after it accused him, in an article titled "The Story of a College Football Fix," of giving football secrets to University of Alabama coach Bear Bryant. Butts was not a public official, but the majority opinion said that his position as a "public figure" required him to show "unreasonable conduct" on the part of the magazine—that is, that the magazine had failed to investigate the story with the ordinary standards followed by publishers.[2] (The Court found that Butts had met that requirement and upheld the $460,000 award that had been granted to him by a lower court.)

The effect of the ruling was to broaden the *Times v. Sullivan* standard to include a new group—"public figures"—that was even more difficult to define than "public officials." By 1971, the Court had included in the definition people who became involved in matters "of public or general interest," even involuntarily. The rationale was that "freedom of discussion, if it would fulfill its historic function in this nation, must embrace all issues about which information is needed or appropriate to enable members of society to cope with the [requirements] of their period."[3] But the standard was so broad, some people felt, that it provided the news media with immunity from libel actions. As a Rhode Island judge remarked in dismissing a libel suit against a newspaper, "What incident covered by a newspaper is not or does not become an event of public interest?"[4]

Then, in a series of cases beginning in 1974, the Supreme Court limited its definition of who might be considered a public figure. A lawyer in a controversial civil case, a scientist who received a government research grant, and a prominent society woman involved in a highly publicized divorce were held to be private individuals largely because they had not sought the limelight, did not seek to influence public opinion, or did not normally hold positions of power or influence. As private individuals, the Court said, they did not have to show actual malice but only negligence to win their cases; and it was left to state courts to determine what constituted negligence.

Shifting Ground. The result of these various rulings is that libel has remained a gray area, and one that continues to raise important issues with respect to freedom of expression. Some people argue that, in granting First Amendment protection (however vague and limited) to certain instances of defamatory speech, the Supreme Court went too far and created a situation in which officials and public figures can be destroyed by hints of scandal in the press. As one such critic describes it:

> *From the moment the allegations are published, the curtain falls. Clients run away, job opportunities vanish, friends are hard to find. . . . Even if [the victims] are eventually "cleared," it is often too late for them to resume their lives at anything like the level at which they functioned prior to the scandals.*[5]

The answer, many people who hold this view say, is to strengthen libel laws and adopt one standard for officials, public figures, and private individuals alike: If a defamatory statement can't be proved true, it's libel.

However, others argue that libel laws already have a "chilling effect" on freedom of expression, limiting the flow of information to the public because newspapers and broadcasters withhold reports that they fear may spark court actions. The fear is understandable; in recent years, juries have tended to award huge amounts, sometimes millions of dollars, in libel cases. Moreover, the cost of mounting a defense against a libel action can easily reach several hundred thousand dollars—even if the suit is groundless and the defense is successful. From this point of view, the answer is to set ceilings on damage awards and clarify, not remove, the First Amendment protections outlined in *Times* v. *Sullivan* and later cases.

Adding to the debate is the question of whether the Constitution guarantees a "right to privacy" and, if so, what relationship that right has to freedom of expression. Although the Constitution contains no specific mention of a right to privacy, several Supreme Court justices have found that it is implied by other provisions, such as the ban on unreasonable searches in the Fourth Amendment. Most states also recognize privacy rights in one form or another.

As changes in the law have made it more difficult to bring libel suits, suits for invasion of privacy have become more common. Disclosing private information about a person can prompt a suit even if the information can be proved true—it's enough that it presents the person in an embarrassing light and serves no legitimate public interest. But here, too, it's not always clear what is and is not legitimate public interest.

Libel and privacy are areas where important rights are in competition—the right to free speech and open debate on the one hand and the rights of an individual to privacy and reputation on the other. The competition is taking place on shifting legal ground, and many questions remain. But these are not the only areas where freedom of expression may be limited by competing rights and concerns, as we shall see.

7

"Second-Class"
Speech

Until June 1990, 2 Live Crew was just one of dozens of musical groups riding the wave of rap music's popularity. But in that month the group achieved national fame. The reason: On June 10, after a performance at a club in Hollywood, Florida, they were arrested and charged with obscenity for the lyrics of their songs. Two days earlier, a Florida record-store owner had been arrested as well, for selling copies of the group's album *Nasty As They Wanna Be.*

Another obscenity case also made national headlines that spring. The Contemporary Arts Center, a museum in Cincinnati, Ohio, was brought to court on obscenity charges for displaying a traveling exhibition of works by the photographer Robert Mapplethorpe. It was the first time a museum had faced such charges for an exhibit.

Meanwhile, debate was growing over an entirely different matter—a movement to restrict cigarette advertising because of tobacco's well-documented harmful effects. New York City, for example, proposed to ban such ads from buses, subways, and city-owned bill-

The rap group 2 Live Crew filed a suit trying to stop obscenity arrests for the sales of their album. Here, Luther Campbell, a member of the group and president of its record label, points to the warning sticker on his shirt, identical to the one on the group's controversial album, Nasty As They Wanna Be.

boards; similar moves were urged in other communities. This was part of a long-simmering controversy; twenty years earlier, Congress had banned cigarette commercials from radio and television, and there had been several attempts to ban such advertising altogether since then.

On the surface this cigarette-ad controversy had nothing to do with the Florida and Cincinnati obscenity trials. But in fact, both involved issues of freedom of expression. Since the framing of the Constitution, the primary reason advanced for the First Amendment's guarantee of freedom of expression has been the need, in a democracy, for unrestricted debate on public affairs—the "uninhibited, robust, and wide-open" debate called for by Justice Brennan in *Times* v. *Sullivan*. But what about speech that has little or nothing to do with public affairs and is considered harmful in some way? Should it be granted the same protection?

Advertising and obscenity are two areas where this question has been raised repeatedly. On the whole, courts have declined to place these forms of expression on a par with political debate, judging them to be what is sometimes called "second-class" speech. But there is controversy and confusion in both areas.

Commercial Speech. Advertising is one of the most closely regulated forms of expression in America. State and federal laws bar false, misleading, and unfair ads; at the national level, the Federal Trade Commission sets standards and enforces the laws.

This regulatory system was put in place in the early 1900s, in response to abuses by companies that made false (sometimes outrageous) claims in their ads. Typical was a late 1800s magazine ad for "Dr. Scott's Electric Corset," which was said to cure weight problems and "any bodily ailment" through electricity and "magnetic power." The ad named doctors (including a former U.S. surgeon general) who supposedly endorsed the product; but no law required the advertiser to get the doctors' permission before listing their names.[1]

Restrictions on false and deceptive ads have never been seriously challenged as restrictions on expression; few people would argue that the First Amendment creates a right to defraud customers. But even truthful, fair advertising has been regulated—with restrictions on forms of advertising, advertising for certain products and services, and advertising directed at certain groups. How do these restrictions square with the First Amendment?

Until 1964, they squared just fine—advertising was held to be "commercial speech," completely outside the amendment's protection. This view was set out in 1942, in the case of a man who bought a used navy submarine and planned to exhibit it in New York City. When he tried to pass out handbills advertising the attraction, he was told that a city ordinance permitted only handbills containing "information or protest"—not commercial ads. His solution was to print a protest on the back of the handbill and try again; but the Supreme Court, ruling in his case, found this a willful attempt to get around the law. And nothing in the Constitution, the Court said, prevented government from regulating "purely commercial advertising."[2]

Then came *Times* v. *Sullivan,* the 1964 case that had such impact in the area of libel. An important factor in this case was the fact that the supposedly libelous statements were contained in a paid advertisement. Did that make them "commercial speech," outside constitutional protection? The Court held that it did not: The ad "communicated information, expressed opinion, recited grievances, protested claimed abuses, and sought financial support on behalf of a movement whose existence and

Health! Comfort! Elegance!

DR. SCOTT'S Electric Corset.

Positively Secured with this

BEAUTIFUL INVENTION

By a happy thought Dr. Scott, of London, the Inventor of the celebrated Electric Brushes, has adapted Electro-Magnetism to Ladies' Corsets, thus bringing this wonderful curative agency within the reach of every lady.

They should be adopted at once by those suffering from any bodily ailment, and she who wishes to

Ward Off Disease,

Preserve her good health, and retain and improve the elegance of her figure should give them an immediate trial. It has been found that magnetic treatment makes the muscles and tissues more plastic and yielding, and it is argued from this that Ladies who wear these corsets will have no difficulty in moulding the figure to any desired form, without tight lacing. A tendency to extreme fatness or leanness is a disease which, in most cases, these articles will be found to cure. In appearance they do not differ from the usual corsets, being made of the same materials and shape (see cut). They are worn the same, and fit the same, but give a more graceful figure.

> The Secretary of the Pall Mall Electric Association of London "earnestly recommends all" "Ladies suffering from any" "bodily ailment to adopt" "these corsets without delay." "They perform astonishing" "cures and invigorate every" "part of the system."

In place of the ordinary steel busks in front, and a rib or two at the back, Dr. Scott inserts steel magnetods which are exactly the same size, shape, length, breadth and thickness as the usual steel busk or rib. By this means he is able to bring the magnetic power into constant contact with all the vital organs, and yet preserve that symmetry and lightness so desirable in a good corset. It is affirmed by professional men that there is hardly a disease which Electricity and Magnetism will not benefit or cure.

Dr. W. A. Hammond, of New York,

Late Surgeon-General of the United States, an eminent authority, publishes almost miraculous cures made by him, and all medical men daily practice the same. Ask your own physician. The sale of Magnetic Clothing, Band, Belts, etc., has attained world-wide success, but many who are constrained to use them are deterred because they are either expensive, bulky, troublesome, or interfere with the dress and figure. The cut gives a fair representation of the corset, which should be worn daily in place of the ordinary one, and will always do good, never harm. There is no shock or sensation whatever felt in wearing them, while benefit quickly foll ws. Being made with better material and workmanship than any corset sold, they will outwear...

Over-enthusiastic ads such as this, for Dr. Scott's Electric Corset, eventually led to restrictions on claims made by advertisers. The Federal Trade Commission decides which claims are acceptable.

objectives are matters of the highest public interest. . . . That the *Times* was paid for the advertisement is as immaterial in this connection as the fact that newspapers and books are sold."[3]

In the years that followed, the distinction between purely commercial advertising (which could be regulated) and advertising that fell into the area of "public interest" (which could not) became increasingly blurred. The Court overruled, for example, state and local restrictions that barred newspapers from running ads for an abortion referral service, pharmacies from advertising their prices for prescription drugs, and lawyers from advertising their regular services. The main reason was that the ads provided information that helped consumers make decisions—and a free flow of information was as important to the U.S. market economy as it was to the democratic political process.

Nothing in these rulings prevented restrictions on false and misleading ads or on illegal ads (such as employment ads that discriminate against women or minorities). And government could still restrict the time, place, and manner of advertising. (Thus bans on cigarette ads on television—or New York City buses—could be enforced.) Nor did the Court put "commercial speech" on a level with political debate. Later cases indicated that ads for products and services could be banned or restricted when doing so served an important public interest. But government would now have to be prepared to show, in court if necessary, that its restrictions directly advanced that interest. Commercial speech, previously outside the First Amendment, had new status.

That status is still unclear, however. For example, in 1987 the Court seemed to reverse its stand, ruling that government could ban or regulate advertising for any product that could itself be regulated. The case involved ads for legal gambling casinos in Puerto Rico, but the principle could apply to a wide range of products and services—not only tobacco and alcohol, but banking, legal and health care services, prescription and nonprescription drugs, and a long list of others. In fact, *any* economic activity can be regulated. Does that mean that government can ban advertising for any product, even when the ads are truthful and the product is legal? Critics of the decision found this disturbing. It would be better, they said, to ban harmful products themselves than to establish a principle that allowed government such broad powers to limit speech.

The debate over advertising shows that the concept of "second-class" commercial speech is a shadowy one—something that is no less true of obscenity.

Obscenity and the Law. Dictionary definitions of "obscene" include "abhorrent to morality or virtue" and "designed to incite to lust or depravity." Pornography, says the dictionary, is "material (as books or a photograph) that depicts erotic behavior and is intended to cause sexual excitement."[4] The definitions themselves point to some of the central problems in this area: Whose standards of "morality" and "virtue" should apply? What constitutes "depravity" or "erotic behavior"? How can intent be judged? For example, is material pornographic if it causes "sexual excitement" but has other purposes as well?

Not surprisingly, views on these questions have changed over the years. In colonial times, Massachusetts banned "filthy, obscene, or profane" material; Vermont, in 1821, was the first state to adopt such a law.[5] But anti-obscenity laws were rare (and even more rarely enforced) until the 1870s, when a number of self-appointed guardians of public morality began to urge stricter controls on material they considered offensive. Among them was Anthony Comstock, who, as secretary of a group called the New York Society for the Suppression of Vice, successfully campaigned for a federal law that imposed stiff fines and prison terms of up to ten years for the mailing of any obscene or "indecent" material. By the turn of the century, most states also had anti-obscenity laws.

Material that ran afoul of these laws was held up to a legal standard that had been imported from English law: If it tended to "deprave and corrupt those whose minds are open to such immoral influences, and into whose hands a publication of this sort might fall," it was obscene. In other words, works were judged by the effects of isolated passages on the most susceptible persons.[6] The result was that people such as Margaret Sanger were prosecuted for providing information on birth control, and various federal, state, and local review boards banned such literary works as Walt Whitman's *Leaves of Grass,* Theodore Dreiser's *American Tragedy,* John Steinbeck's *Grapes of Wrath* and *East of Eden,* and James Joyce's *Ulysses.*

Courts were already backing away from this strict standard when, in 1957, a New York publisher and bookseller named Samuel Roth was convicted of violating the 1873 federal law by mailing obscene books and other materials. He appealed his case, and for the first time the Supreme Court found itself presented with the issue of obscenity.

The Court upheld Roth's conviction 6–3; the majority opinion, by Justice Brennan, said that obscenity was simply outside the protection of the First Amendment because it was lacking in "redeeming social importance." But in the same ruling, the Court set a new standard for judging obscene material. The old rule, Brennan said, was too rigorous—"judging obscenity by the effect of isolated passages upon the most susceptible persons, might well encompass material legitimately treating with sex," and sex and obscenity were not the same. Instead, the standard should be "whether to the average person, applying contemporary community standards, the dominant theme of the material taken as a whole appeals to prurient interest" (or "excites lustful thoughts").[7]

The new standard presented some problems of its own, not the least of which was that of defining "contemporary community standards." Seven years later the Court took up the question again in the case of a theater manager convicted under an Ohio law that barred the showing of obscene films, and Brennan attempted to clarify the *Roth* standard. First, he said, obscene material had to be "utterly without redeeming social importance"—if it advocated ideas or had literary, artistic, or scientific value, or any other form of social importance, it could not be denied constitutional protection. In addition, "contemporary community standards" were *national,* not local, standards. "It is, after all, a national Constitution we are expounding," he said.[8]

While the Court overturned the theater manager's conviction, only Justice Arthur Goldberg went along entirely with Brennan's view. Instead, the case produced five separate opinions. Justices Black and Douglas held that any restrictions on obscenity were on weak ground because they were in effect restrictions on thought and thus couldn't be squared with the First Amendment (they had dissented for the same reason in *Roth*). Justices John Marshall Harlan and Tom Clark and Chief Justice Earl F. Warren would have left the matter of obscenity up to the states to varying degrees. And Justice Potter Stewart argued that only hard-core pornography should be pun-

Cartoonist Mike Smith expresses his concern over the definition of obscenity. Restrictions could eliminate hard-core pornography, but the process could indiscriminately eliminate all magazines that feature nudity in any form.

ished. To the question of what "hard-core pornography" might be, he said, "I know it when I see it."[9]

Through the 1960s and early 1970s, the Court continued to air these differing views as it tried to refine the *Roth* standard in a series of cases*—with what seemed to be a growing sense of frustration. Wrote Justice Black: "As the Court's many decisions in this area demonstrate, it is extremely difficult for judges or any other citizens to agree on what is 'obscene.'"[10] In fact, courts were struggling with the issue of obscenity at the same time that public views on sex and morality were undergoing sweeping changes—changes that some people hailed as new freedom and others viewed as excessive permissiveness. Where did obscenity and pornography fit in this rapidly changing picture? In general, conservatives argued for tighter restrictions, while liberals urged broader First Amendment protection. But many feminists, who otherwise counted themselves among liberals, sided with conservatives on this issue, arguing that pornography demeans women and may even encourage sexual abuse.

Arguably, the legal confusion over obscenity only reflected the confusion of Americans in general. By 1973, however, the makeup of the Court had changed to include four justices who held more conservative views: Chief Justice Warren E. Burger and associate justices Harry A. Blackmun, Lewis F. Powell, and William H. Rehnquist. And in that year, the Court made major changes in the obscenity standard.

---

*Notably *"Memoirs of a Woman of Pleasure"* v. *Massachusetts,* 383 U.S. 413, in which the Court cleared the eighteenth-century novel *Fanny Hill* of criminal charges and set up a three-part test in which material had to be proved "utterly" without social importance to be judged obscene.

The* Miller *Standard. The case that prompted the changes was *Miller* v. *California,* which involved a man convicted for distributing brochures advertising "adult" books. In essence, the Court threw out the earlier requirement that obscene material had to be proved "utterly without redeeming social importance." Instead, it set up a three-part test: First, would the average person, applying contemporary community standards, find that the work as a whole appealed to prurient interest? Second, did the work depict or describe, in a "patently offensive" way, sexual conduct specifically described by state law? If the work met the first two standards, the third part of the test would be applied: It must have "*serious* literary, artistic, political, or scientific value to merit First Amendment protection"[11] (emphasis added).

However, the new *Miller* test did no better than the old one when it came to defining obscenity. Justice Brennan, who dissented from the ruling, wrote:

> *After fifteen years of experimentation and debate I am reluctantly forced to the conclusion that none of the available formulas, including the one announced today, can reduce the vagueness to a tolerable level. . . . Any effort to draw a constitutionally acceptable boundary on state power must resort to such indefinite concepts as "prurient interest," "patent offensiveness," "serious literary value," and the like. The meaning of these concepts necessarily varies with the experience, outlook, and even idiosyncrasies of the person defining them.*[12]

At the same time, the Court reversed its stand on "community standards," holding that local, not national, standards should apply. This raised troubling questions. Material that was acceptable in one area might now be illegal in another. As a result, many books and films might not be produced, for fear of violating standards in conservative communities. In short, the fear was that standards would be set by the most sensitive sectors of society, as they had been a hundred years before. Critics of the Court decision predicted a flood of cases.

While dozens of cases have come to court since the *Miller* decision, the results have not been as drastic as some of the critics feared. The 2 Live Crew and Mapplethorpe cases provide good examples. The rap group was acquitted—the jury in the case found that their songs, which described explicit sexual acts and referred to women in demeaning sexual terms, were a legitimate form of social and even political comment. One juror remarked that the group's lyrics were "just not obscene. People in everyday society use those words."[13] But the record-store owner who sold the group's album was convicted; in that case, a federal judge had previously ruled that the album was obscene. (The rap group filed a lawsuit to prevent further arrests.)

The Mapplethorpe case involved 7 of the 175 photographs that were in the exhibit. Most of them depicted nude figures in poses that the jurors agreed were grotesque and disgusting. But they accepted the view of experts who testified to the artistic merit of the photographs, and the museum was acquitted. In short, the pictures met the first two parts of the *Miller* test but not the third.

Questions about obscenity continue to create controversy, especially in the field of broadcasting. The Federal Communications Commission, which regulates radio and television broadcasters, has long held them to strict standards; stations can lose their licenses for airing material deemed "offensive" or "indecent" by the FCC code. The reasoning behind this is that broadcasts may reach "unwilling" listeners, including children. Even so, the FCC has allowed offensive material to be broadcast late at night, on the theory that children won't be listening then. In 1988, Congress ordered the FCC to impose a round-the-clock ban on this material. But the new rule was challenged, and in 1991 a federal appeals court ruled that such a ban would violate the First Amendment.

Another controversy surrounds federal funding for the arts. Conservatives, led by Republican senator Jesse Helms and by such groups as the American Family Association (headed by the Protestant minister Donald E. Wildmon), have attacked the National Endowment for the Arts (a federal agency that funds artistic programs) for issuing grants to projects they consider offensive. As a result, the NEA changed its procedures for issuing grants in 1990. The long-term effects of the change, if any, were unclear; but many artists were disturbed by the idea of political groups attempting to set artistic standards.

In fact, as Justice Brennan warned, assessing artistic, literary, and social value has proved a highly subjective business. Nude dancing in a nightclub may be (and has been) ruled obscene; but does that mean that any on-stage nudity can be banned? If not, what circumstances make it acceptable? Does a book or a painting lack social value if the majority of people in a town would say so, even if most people in the next town would not? Years after *Miller,* the Court was still struggling with this question. In 1987, it ruled that social value should be judged by the standards of a "reasonable person" rather than a majority of a community.[14] But even "reasonable" people can disagree in these matters.

A Pandora's Box? Some people believe that, in designating areas of "second-class" speech with partial First

Amendment protection, the Supreme Court has opened up a Pandora's box. The difficulties in defining what is and is not acceptable, and what may and may not be restricted, seem nearly endless. The Court's legal reasoning is not always easy to follow, either. For example, in an opinion upholding a town's right to regulate "adult" theaters through zoning regulations, Justice John Paul Stevens wrote:

> [F]ew of us would march our sons and daughters off to war to preserve the citizen's right to see "Specified Sexual Activities" exhibited in the theaters of our choice. Even though the First Amendment protects communication in this area from total suppression, we hold that the State may legitimately use the content of these materials as the basis for placing them in a different classification from other motion pictures.[15]

But as one legal scholar pointed out:

> Few of us would march our sons or daughters off to war to preserve the citizen's right to see pictures of American Nazis marching in uniform in Skokie, Illinois, or to hear advocacy of Stalinist Communism, or to read advertisements stating the price of prescription drugs. That test is both unreasoning and insufficient.[16]

As long as restrictions on "second-class" speech are based on attempts to weigh the content of the material and balance its value against competing social interests, such debates are likely to continue.

8

Speech in the Schools

Do school officials have the right to censor a student newspaper? Can they control what students and teachers say, in or out of class? Ban books from the school library?

Some of the most heated arguments over freedom of expression in America have taken place in the public schools. In a way, a school is a small version of society—with its own citizens (students), government (teachers and administrators), and social and political concerns. But several features set schools apart from the rest of society. One obvious difference is that schools exist for the specific purpose of educating children. Another is that public schools receive government funds—tax dollars—to carry out this purpose. And while private schools are an option for some families, most parents must send their children to public schools, to be exposed to whatever they find there. Do these factors change the ground rules where freedom of expression is concerned?

Many people have argued that they do. If schools are to educate children, the argument goes, they must be able to control what students see and hear and, to some degree, say. A closely related idea is the belief that children are impressionable and need to be protected from "harmful" views and ideas. Moreover, the taxpayers who fund public schools should not be expected to see their money used to spread ideas they find repugnant.

But others argue that expression should be no less open in schools than in the rest of society. Censorship in the schools, they say, both denies students a basic right and sets a bad example, indicating that restrictions on speech are acceptable. Besides, when students are not exposed to competing views in school, how will they learn to function in a democracy? As one journalist put it, "If freedom of expression becomes merely an empty slogan in the minds of enough children, it will be dead by the time they are adults."[1]

Student Speech. For much of American history, the idea that educators could control speech in schools was accepted; questions about freedom of expression began to come up only in the twentieth century. An important principle was established in 1943 when the Supreme Court ruled that public school students could not be compelled to salute the American flag. The case (*West Virginia State Board of Education* v. *Barnette*) had been brought by members of the Jehovah's Witnesses, who said that saluting the flag violated their religious principles. While the case involved a conflict between religion and government, the Supreme Court based its ruling on the broad issue of freedom of expression. Politics and religion were matters of opinion, the Court said; no official could decree what opinion was orthodox and force citizens to swear to it. The Court saw no reason to treat students differently.

However, to *compel* speech is one thing; to *control* it, by limiting what students write and say, is another. Such limits weren't seriously challenged until the 1960s, when many students (in high schools as well as colleges) became involved in protests against the Vietnam War. Then, in December 1965, a group of students in Des Moines, Iowa, took part in a protest that ended up breaking new constitutional ground. The protest was subdued: The students simply wore black armbands to symbolize their opposition to the war. But Des Moines school officials said that political protests had no place in their schools, and they suspended three students—John Tinker, age fifteen, Mary Beth Tinker, age thirteen, and Christopher Eckhardt, age sixteen—who refused to remove the armbands.

The students took their case to court, and it reached the Supreme Court in 1969. By a vote of 7–2, the Court ruled that the school officials had overstepped their bounds by forbidding an action (wearing armbands) that was a clear expression of a political idea. In the majority opinion, written by Justice Abe Fortas, the Court said:

> It can hardly be argued that either students or teachers shed their rights at the schoolhouse gate. . . . In our system, state-operated schools may not be enclaves of totalitarianism. School officials do not possess absolute authority over their students. Students in school as well as out of school are 'persons' under our Constitution. . . . Students may not be regarded as closed-circuit recipients of only that which the State wishes to communicate. They may not be confined to the expression of those sentiments that are officially approved.[2]

The Court acknowledged that there were circumstances in which student expression could be limited—for example, if a student disrupted classwork, created "substantial disor-

Mary Beth Tinker and her brother, John, display the armbands they wore to protest the Vietnam War and to mourn the war dead. The U.S. Supreme Court ruled in favor of the students' right to wear the bands despite the opposition of school officials.

der," or infringed on the rights of others. But these circumstances did not exist in the *Tinker* case, and the fact that school officials feared the armbands *might* cause a disturbance was not enough, the Court said:

> *Any departure from absolute regimentation may cause trouble. Any variation from the majority's opinion may inspire fear. Any word spoken, in class, in the lunchroom or on the campus, that deviates from the views of another person, may start an argument or cause a disturbance. But our Constitution says we must take this risk.*

Because it extended the First Amendment's free-speech protection to students in school, the *Tinker* decision was seen as a landmark. It was also controversial. Among those who voiced strong disagreement was Justice Black, one of the two justices who dissented in the ruling. Black was an ardent supporter of free speech but drew a sharp line between the right to express ideas (which he felt was absolute) and the freedom to express those ideas at any time or in any place or manner (which he felt could be restricted). Schools were within their rights to restrict student expression, he said; not to do so would be to "surrender control of the American public school to public school students."[3]

Despite the controversy, it seemed for several years that the principle behind the majority opinion in *Tinker* would stand. Then, in the 1980s, two cases called that principle into question. By this time, the mood of the country as a whole was more conservative; in addition, the Supreme Court included more conservative members. And on the question of speech in the schools, as on the question of obscenity, the court seemed to draw back from the broad freedom it had outlined in the 1960s.

The first case, which reached the Supreme Court in 1986, was *Bethel School District* v. *Matthew Fraser.* Fraser, a high school senior, had delivered a speech nominating a friend for student-government office in which he made a number of thinly disguised sexual references. Although the metaphors he used could hardly be considered obscene, a majority of the Court said that school officials were justified in taking disciplinary action against him because students' First Amendment rights did not extend to "indecent" speech that might disrupt a school assembly.

In the second case, *Hazelwood School District* v. *Kuhlmeier,* the Court said that school officials had broad powers to censor school newspapers, plays, and other activities. This case began in 1983, when a high school principal in Hazelwood, Missouri, deleted two pages in the student newspaper, *Spectrum.* The pages in question contained articles on teenage pregnancy and divorce that the principal said were "inappropriate." Cathy Kuhlmeier and two other students appealed in court, and the Supreme Court ruled on the case in early 1988.[4]

In effect, the school had exercised prior restraint by preventing publication of the stories. That was something that government had been barred from doing, except in the most extreme circumstances, for more than half a century. But a majority of the justices said the school was within its rights in censoring the paper. For one thing, the school sponsored this paper; students were graded on and received academic credit for work on it, and stories were assigned and edited by a teacher. Thus opinions in the paper might be seen as having the approval of the school—and the school couldn't be required to endorse material it considered inappropriate.

But the Court went beyond the idea that a school could control the content of a newspaper that, in essence,

The Hazelwood East High School principal holds a copy of the school newspaper after the Supreme Court ruled that high school journalists do not always have the same First Amendment protection as adults.

it owned and published. The majority opinion, by Justice Byron White, suggested that schools would be justified in censoring any form of expression that related to legitimate teaching concerns and educational goals. The ruling sparked a stinging dissent from Justices Brennan, Marshall, and Blackmun, who said that it contradicted *Tinker*. They feared that, under the broad, vague criteria set out by the majority, school officials might censor any views that did not fit with their own, producing "thought control in the high school." Besides, the dissenters pointed out, there were far less oppressive ways for school officials to disassociate themselves from the opinions in a student newspaper (they could, for example, print a disclaimer in each issue). "The young men and women of Hazelwood East expected a civics lesson," Brennan wrote, "but not the one the Court teaches them today."[5]

Hazelwood also provoked a general outcry from press groups and civil rights advocates. "Now just about any educational reason will justify heavy editing and outright exclusion of student articles," said a *New York Times* editorial.[6] Decrying the lesson that students would learn from the ruling, author Nat Hentoff wrote, "If those Americans who are now in school do not come to see the First Amendment as a *personal* liberty, worth fighting for, then no written constitution can save it."[7]

No matter how one views *Fraser* and *Hazelwood,* they clearly show that student speech can be restricted by school officials. How far officials can go in imposing restrictions is far less clear, however.

Hate Speech on Campus. One of the disturbing trends of the late 1980s and early 1990s was a resurgence of racism in the United States. Among the places where this trend surfaced were colleges and universities, which were faced with a growing number of racial incidents (a reported seventy-eight in one semester of 1988 alone). In response, many university officials adopted anti-harassment codes—and in the process renewed the debate about free speech in schools.

Most of these codes barred spoken, written, and symbolic attacks based on race, ethnic origin, color, sex, religion, sexual orientation, or handicaps. Some were based on the old concept of "fighting words"—they banned insults that were directed at individuals or small groups and were likely to cause a violent reaction. Others were much broader, forbidding even general negative remarks. In fact, in 1989 a federal court ordered the University of Michigan to change its code because it was so broad and vague that it was unconstitutional.

At Brown University, after racist graffiti and white supremacist leaflets were found in a dormitory, officials adopted a code that made it unacceptable to subject "another person, group, or class of persons to inappropriate, abusive, threatening or demeaning actions based on race, religion, gender, handicap, ethnicity, national origin or sexual orientation."[8] In 1991, a student was expelled for violating this code. It was the first such action at any university, and it focused national attention on both the problem of campus racism and the free speech question involved.

The student, who had been drinking (also a violation of campus rules), had shouted anti-black, anti-Jewish, and anti-homosexual remarks in the courtyard of a dormitory. It was the second time he had been charged with breaking the code. Neither he nor university officials would discuss the specifics of the case with the press, but he told reporters that his expulsion was a "political statement by the university" and that he would pursue the case as a violation of the First Amendment.[9]

Are schools within their rights in banning "hate speech"? There are strong arguments on each side. Few people would question a school's right to forbid actions that lead to violence. Certainly it's in the interest of a school—and society as a whole—to promote tolerance and combat racism. Racist speech might fall outside First Amendment protection, some people hold, because it interferes with the rights of minorities to be treated equally. And at a private university, such as Brown, school officials may have broader leeway in restricting speech than officials at public (government-run) universities enjoy.

But critics of campus speech codes charge that they have been used to suppress not just "fighting words" but any opinion that is judged not to be "politically correct." For example, the campus radio station at the University of Kansas was forbidden to interview a leader of the Ku Klux Klan. The editor and art director of the student newspaper at the University of California at Los Angeles were suspended after the paper ran a cartoon satirizing affirmative action programs in nonracial terms; when the student paper at California State University at Northridge ran an editorial criticizing the UCLA suspensions, its opinion-page editor was suspended, too.[10]

Besides the potential for abuse, the "hate speech" codes have another drawback: They allow those who make insulting and derogatory remarks to defend them on constitutional grounds. Like many free speech questions, this one has no easy answer.

Censoring Books. Limiting speech is only one of the First Amendment issues that involve education. For years, there have been attempts to restrict books—in public libraries as well as classrooms and school libraries—that were seen as objectionable for one reason or another. Back in the late 1800s, when groups such as Anthony Comstock's New

York Society for the Suppression of Vice were active, libraries often responded to public pressure by banning from their shelves books that seem entirely innocent today. Mark Twain's *Adventures of Huckleberry Finn,* for example, was barred from the Concord Public Library for "a very low grade of morality" and "a systematic use of bad grammar."[11] (Twain is said to have remarked that the banning would ensure sales of 25,000 copies.) Other libraries banned all novels from their shelves.

The 1970s and 1980s, however, produced what some people saw as an "epidemic" of efforts to censor books and other materials in the schools.[12] The school board in Anchorage, Alaska, for example, banned the American Heritage Dictionary in 1976 because it contained such "offensive" words as *tail, ball, nut, ass,* and *bed.*[13] By the early 1980s, according to the citizens' group People for the American Way, such efforts were under way in forty-eight states. Many were led by conservative political groups, but liberals were behind others. *Huckleberry Finn* came under attack again, for example—this time for alleged racism rather than bad grammar.

In a case that focused national attention on the problem, the Island Trees school board, on Long Island, New York, ordered nine books removed from school library shelves after a conservative parents' group objected to them. The books included *Slaughterhouse-Five* by Kurt Vonnegut, *The Fixer* by Bernard Malamud, *The Naked Ape* by Desmond Morris, *Go Ask Alice* by an anonymous author, and *Soul on Ice* by Eldridge Cleaver, as well as other books by black writers and several collections of short stories and essays. The school board called the books "anti-American, anti-Christian, anti-Semitic, and just plain filthy" and said that it acted to protect children from "moral danger."[14]

The celebration and affirmation of the ideals expressed in the First Amendment is the theme for Banned Books Week. Organizations such as the American Library Association, the American Booksellers Association, and the Library of Congress Center for the Book have joined together to produce programs, and materials for the annual observance. The sponsors feel that restraints on the availability of books are far more dangerous than any ideas books may contain.

The reason this action won national attention was that five students sued the school board, claiming that it had violated their First Amendment rights. At first, a federal district court granted summary judgment in favor of the school board. Summary judgment is a decision without a trial; in this case, the court said, there was no need for a trial because the board was entirely within its rights in removing the books. But the students appealed, and the appeals court agreed that there should be a trial. So did a majority of the U.S. Supreme Court, which reviewed the case in 1982 as *Island Trees Board of Education* v. *Pico.*

However, the Supreme Court's 5–4 decision simply indicated that some First Amendment rights were involved; it didn't define those rights. Instead of a single majority opinion, the justices issued several opinions. Three said that schools had virtually absolute discretion to choose classroom materials, but in the library a spirit of free inquiry should hold sway. Four agreed that school boards could remove library books that were vulgar or not suitable from an educational standpoint but could not exercise that power for narrow political reasons, to deny students access to ideas that board members disagreed with. Thus the case didn't produce clear guidelines that school boards (or lower courts) could use in the future.

The standards for selecting books in school classrooms and libraries continue to be debated, and that debate has extended to public libraries as well. Arguably, some form of censorship takes place every time a school or library adds one book, and not another, to its collection. The question is, What standards should be used to make the choice? Some conservative groups have argued that public libraries, which receive public funds, should reflect "majority values." The conservative activist Phyllis Schlafly, for instance, writes that "schools should have a decent respect for the parents' beliefs and attitudes" and that the public "has the right to question whether any preemptive censorship is carried out on the basis of the personal political biases of the librarian or teacher" in choosing books.[15]

On the other hand, the American Library Association (ALA) has endorsed standards that call for librarians to "make available the widest diversity of views and expressions, including those which are unorthodox or unpopular with the majority." The ALA's "Freedom to Read" statement, adopted in 1952 and subsequently revised, echoes the "marketplace of ideas" concept set out by John Milton in the 1600s: "The power of a democratic system to adapt to change is vastly strengthened by the freedom of its citizens to choose widely from among conflicting opinions offered freely to them." Neither majority opinion, nor the personal political views of the librarian, nor the political affiliations of the author are suitable standards for judging a book, the statement says. "No group has the right . . . to impose its own concept of politics or morality upon other members of a democratic society. Freedom is no freedom if it is accorded only to the accepted and the inoffensive."[16]

Academic Freedom. Along with attempts to restrict books and limit student expression, the history of American education is filled with attempts to control the views expressed by teachers in class—and sometimes outside class as well. For many years it was accepted that teachers, because of the importance of their job, should conform to higher standards than average citizens and even give up some basic constitutional rights, such as the right to take part in political activity. Since the 1950s, however, courts have established clearer rights for teachers. Teachers can't, for example, be required to sign loyalty oaths or pledge allegiance to the flag. They can't be dismissed for belonging to a political group, expressing their political views, or raising controversial issues in class—as long as they do so in a spirit of inquiry and debate and do not try to win converts to one political view.

Yet there are limits to what teachers can say or do in class. Courts, in deciding such cases, have weighed such factors as the age of children being taught, the educational value and factual accuracy of the material presented, and the teacher's methods—for example, whether the teacher presented an unbiased selection of evidence. Moreover, teachers continue to face the same pressures (from both conservative and liberal groups) that would limit student expression and restrict access to books.

The questions about freedom of speech in schools—whether they concern teachers, students, or books in the library—boil down to an underlying question about the role education should play. Part of that role in any society is clearly to impart "community values" to young people, and restricting speech may serve that goal. But schools in a democracy are expected to do more than simply hand down the accepted wisdom of the majority. They must teach students to think, to sort through complicated arguments and detect flaws and contradictions, to make decisions. No matter how well intentioned, attempts to screen students from "dangerous" and "offensive" views ultimately work against this goal. In schools no less than in society as a whole, "the answer to a bad idea is a good one."[17]

New
Challenges

Perhaps the most remarkable aspect of freedom of speech in America is that the concept has survived so many challenges since it was first set out more than two hundred years ago. Madison and company would be pleased; they believed that a free flow of information and opinion would be the greatest guarantee of the democracy they created, and so it has proved to be.

It's only necessary to look at some other societies to see that this is so. Dictators and leaders of totalitarian regimes know full well that free speech is the greatest threat to their power; that is why the Nazis staged massive public book burnings when they seized power in Germany before World War II, why the Soviet Communist government controlled and censored the media, and why the first step of any coup is nearly always to take over broadcast stations and newspapers. It is why, hundreds of years ago, the Catholic Church pursued heretics through the Inquisition; and why, in our time, the Ayatollah Khomeini, the fundamentalist Islamic leader of Iran, called for the death of the British writer Salman

Rushdie on the ground that his book *The Satanic Verses* was offensive to Islam. (The death threat was issued in 1989; Rushdie was still in hiding, protected by the British secret service, in 1992.)

Even countries with democratic traditions often control speech more strictly than the United States. The British Official Secrets Act, for instance, makes it a crime for newspapers or broadcasters to disclose any information the government considers sensitive. (Contrast that with the Pentagon Papers case, in which the U.S. government's attempt to stop newspapers from publishing information not only failed, but penalties against the newspapers were never contemplated.) Beginning in 1988, Britain, which has no written constitution, also barred broadcasters from conducting live interviews with members or supporters of the Irish Republican Army, the militant underground group that opposes British rule in Northern Ireland.

But along with the remarkable freedom in the United States has come excess—sleazy headlines in supermarket tabloids; music and films that shock even hardened sensibilities; pornography; publications that spread racist, sexist, and anti-Semitic ideas. In our rights-conscious society, these excesses and extremes are often seen as infringing on other rights: the right to privacy, the right of parents to educate their children, the rights of women and minorities to fair and equal treatment.

Increasingly, there are calls to balance these rights against the right of free speech; and courts have shown some willingness to take this route. For example, a court may limit press coverage of pre-trial proceedings or, in rare cases, a trial itself to guarantee fair treatment of a criminal defendant. And as we have seen, court rulings have created categories—"second class" speech, speech in a school setting, speech that may harm national secu-

Our inability to agree on or even to define obscenity has some negative side effects, in that the First Amendment's protection of expression allows publications and activities that would be considered sordid by the vast majority of citizens.

rity, and so on—in which expression may be restricted to one degree or another, depending on the specific content and circumstances of the case. In these categories, it often falls to judges to weigh the merits of various interests and determine if they outweigh free speech rights.

As deplorable as the excesses are, however, limits on speech ultimately strike at the heart of democracy. The First Amendment is not the property of the right or the left; nor have attempts to limit free speech come exclusively from one political viewpoint or the other. But limits urged by one group can apply to all—if it is justifiable to ban neo-Nazi rhetoric today, then it may be justifiable to ban anti-Nazi rhetoric tomorrow. Once established, principles used to limit speech can be applied in unforeseen ways.

New challenges are certain to arise. Some are already on the horizon. For example, does a computerized message (or "electronic mail") service have a right to censor messages sent by its subscribers, as some have already done? The question may not seem pressing; but if electronic mail becomes the mass method of communication that some people predict it will, free speech and public debate could be limited.

Perhaps the most chilling new attack on free speech is in the area of government funding. In 1988, the Reagan administration imposed a "gag rule" on health clinics that receive government funds, forbidding workers at those clinics from mentioning abortion or even referring women to doctors who would discuss it. In making this rule, the administration reinterpreted a 1970 law that said federal money was not to be used for abortions. The new interpretation was challenged, and in May 1991 the Supreme Court ruled 5–4 (in *Rust* v. *Sullivan*) that the administration was within its rights—even though nothing in the law mandated a gag rule and even though the rule prevented health clinics from giving their patients truthful information about a legal, constitutionally protected option.

The ruling was seen by many as a serious blow for women—"bad medicine and poor public policy" was how one member of Congress described it. "It says that women are not entitled to truth and honesty and fairness."[1] But it was no less serious a blow for free speech because, in effect, the Court established a new principle: Government can control speech wherever government funds are used. And government funds go to universities, museums, scientific research centers, and other facilities all over the country.

How will this principle be applied in the future? "It will not stop with abortion," one observer remarked a few months after the ruling. "Already a Justice Department lawyer has said that when Government aids any private institution, it can direct what may or may not be said there."[2] Some people have warned that *Rust* v. *Sullivan* shows a new, disturbing trend—that the Supreme Court can no longer be counted on to protect freedom of expression. In that case, the focus may shift to the courts and constitutions of individual states.

Yet, outside the press and supporters of women's rights, few people remarked on this new principle. Perhaps few were aware of it. But Americans are, in fact, much more likely to support freedom of expression in the abstract than they are when specific cases arise. Various studies have shown, for example, that less than half of all Americans think unpopular opinions should not be banned outright by the majority, that only a third believe high school teachers have a right to express opinions that go against community standards, that some forty-six percent would grant to a federal board of censors the power to decide which television programs can or cannot be shown.[3]

"Give me the liberty to know, to utter, to argue freely according to conscience, above all liberties," John Milton wrote in 1644.[4] But today, as former Supreme Court justice Arthur Goldberg warned in 1980, "We are again becoming intolerant of dissenting voices, forgetful that our nation was founded and forged by dissenters and that while [dissenters] are often misguided, on occasion they are right."[5]

The history of freedom of expression in America shows that it has never been easy to apply the abstract concept to real situations, where competing interests and strong emotions come into play. "Our own interests are so personal to each of us that it is often extremely difficult to appreciate a problem in the light of the interests of others," Chief Justice Earl Warren once wrote. "Yet, this is what we must do. . . . There are neither rights nor freedoms in any meaningful sense unless they can be enjoyed by all." Reviewing the atrocities committed by the Nazis of Hitler, the Fascists of Mussolini, and the Communists of Stalin, Warren noted:

> *The important thing to remember is that in none of these countries were these cruelties put upon the people by foreign conquerers. They were initiated and executed by their own leaders when the people abandoned to them the unbridled power to rule. . . . Thus, it was the evasion of responsibility—not the subjugation by force—that led to the erosion of rights and, eventually, to cataclysmic disaster.*[6]

Freedom of expression is the core value of democracy. When we allow it to be limited—no matter how necessary or well-meaning the limits seem—we do so at our peril. As the eighteenth-century British statesman William Pitt observed, "Necessity is the plea for every infringement of human freedom. It is the argument of tyrants; it is the creed of slaves."[7]

Notes

Court decisions and opinions are referenced here according to the uniform system developed by the Harvard Law Review Association. A citation such as *Cohen v. California,* 403 U.S. 15 (1971), means that the case was decided in 1971 and is reported in *United States Reports,* volume 403, page 15.

Chapter One

1. *The New York Times,* June 22, 1989, p. A1.
2. *The New York Times,* June 22, 1989, p. B8.
3. Marc A. Franklin, *The First Amendment and the Fourth Estate* (New York: Foundation Press, 1981), p. 34.

Chapter Two

1. Euripides, *The Suppliants,* quoted in *John Milton: Complete Poems and Major Prose,* ed. Merritt Y. Hughes (Indianapolis: Bobbs-Merrill, 1957), p. 716.
2. John Milton, *Areopagitica,* in Hughes, pp. 717–49.
3. Edwin Emery, *The Press and America: An Interpretive History of the Mass Media* (Englewood Cliffs, N.J.: Prentice-Hall, 1972), p. 20.

4. Emery, p. 28.
5. Quoted in William Francois, *Mass Media Law and Regulation* (Columbus, Ohio: Grid, 1978), p. 3.
6. Emery, pp. 63–64.
7. William O. Douglas, *The Right of the People* (New York: Doubleday, 1958), p. 38.
8. Franklin, p. 12.
9. Francois, p. 15.
10. Quoted in Milton Meltzer, *The Bill of Rights: How We Got It and What It Means* (New York: Thomas Y. Crowell, 1990), p. 49.
11. Publius, "On Alleged Defects in the Constitution," *The Federalist Papers,* 1788; quoted in *Civil Liberties: Opposing Viewpoints,* ed. Julie S. Bach (San Diego: Greenhaven Press, 1988), pp. 35–36. The essay is generally attributed to Hamilton.
12. Quoted in Bach, p. 35.
13. Quoted in Nat Hentoff, *The First Freedom: The Tumultuous History of Free Speech in America* (New York: Delacorte Press, 1988), p. 74.
14. Quoted in Hentoff, p. 75.

Chapter Three

1. The *Aurora* (*Philadelphia General Advertiser*), December 23, 1796, quoted in Emery, p. 118.
2. U.S. Statutes at Large, I, Sec. 2, p. 596. Quoted in Emery, p. 121.
3. Quoted in Herbert McClosky and Alida Brill, *Dimensions of Tolerance: What Americans Believe About Civil Liberties* (New York: Russell Sage Foundation, 1983), p. 40.
4. Quoted in Emery, p. 132.
5. Calder M. Pickett, ed. *Voices of the Past: Key Documents in the History of American Journalism* (Columbus, Ohio: Grid), p. 117.
6. Hentoff, p. 104.
7. Emery, p. 516.
8. Emery, p. 517.
9. *Schenck* v. *United States*, 249 U.S. 47 (1919).

10. Fred W. Friendly, *The Constitution—That Delicate Balance* (New York: Random House, 1984), p. 77.
11. *Abrams* v. *United States,* 250 U.S. 616 (1919).
12. Friendly, p. 38.
13. *Near* v. *Minnesota,* 283 U.S. 697 (1931).
14. Friendly, p. 72.
15. Friendly, p. 82.
16. Friendly, p. 83.
17. Friendly, p. 86.

Chapter Four

1. Archibald Cox, in *Harvard Law Review* 94:1 (1980), p. 42.
2. *Chaplinsky* v. *New Hampshire,* 315 U.S. 83 (1942).
3. *Terminiello* v. *City of Chicago,* 337 U.S. 1 (1949).
4. *Cohen* v. *California,* 403 U.S. 15 (1971).
5. Cox, p. 42. Cox cites *Gooding* v. *Wilson,* 405 U.S. 519 (1972), and *Brown* v. *Oklahoma,* 408 U.S. 914 (1972).
6. Alan Brinkly, "Old Glory: The Saga of a National Love Affair," *The New York Times,* July 1, 1990, p. E2.
7. *Spence* v. *Washington,* 418 U.S. 405 (1974).
8. Tamar Lewin, "Hate Crime Law Is Focus of Case on Free Speech," *The New York Times,* December 1, 1991, p. 1.
9. Ibid.
10. Ibid.
11. Ibid.

Chapter Five

1. See Emery, pp. 507–28.
2. Quoted in Curtis D. MacDougall, *Newsroom Problems and Policies* (New York: Dover Books, 1963), p. 263.
3. These and other examples are cited by MacDougall, pp. 264–65.
4. Quoted in MacDougall, p. 268.
5. Quoted in Friendly, p. 51.
6. Quoted in MacDougall, p. 269.

7. For an account of the press role in the Vietnam War, see Peter Braestrup, *Big Story* (Garden City, N.Y.: Anchor Books, 1978).
8. Benjamin C. Bradlee, *The Washington Post National Weekly Edition,* June 23, 1986; reprinted in *The Mass Media: Opposing Viewpoints,* ed. Neal Bernards (San Diego: Greenhaven Press, 1988), p. 101.
9. *New York Times Company* v. *United States* and *United States* v. *The Washington Post Company,* 403 U.S. 713 (1971).
10. Ibid.
11. James Madison, letter to W. T. Barry, quoted by Douglas in *Environmental Protection Agency* v. *Mink,* 410 U.S. 73 (1973).

Chapter Six

1. *New York Times* v. *Sullivan,* 376 U.S. 254 (1964).
2. *Curtis Publishing Co.* v. *Butts* and *Associated Press* v. *Walker,* 388 U.S. 130 (1967).
3. *Rosenbloom* v. *Metromedia,* 403 U.S. 29 (1971).
4. Chief U.S. District Court Judge Raymond Pettine, quoted in Francois, p. 109.
5. Michael Ledeen, "The New McCarthyism," in *Censorship: Opposing Viewpoints,* ed. Lisa Orr (San Diego: Greenhaven Press, 1990), p. 80.

Chapter Seven

1. Franklin, p. 260.
2. *Valentine* v. *Chrestensen,* 316 U.S. 52 (1942).
3. *Times* v. *Sullivan,* 376 U.S. 254 (1964).
4. Definitions in *Webster's Ninth New Collegiate Dictionary* (Springfield, Mass.: Merriam-Webster, 1983).
5. Francois, p. 356.
6. Francois, p. 356-57.
7. *Samuel Roth* v. *U.S.* and *David S. Alberts* v. *State of California,* 354 U.S. 476 (1957).
8. *Jacobellis* v. *State of Ohio,* 378 U.S. 184 (1964).

9. Ibid.

10. *U.S.* v. *Reidel,* 402 U.S. 351 (1971).

11. *Miller* v. *California,* 413 U.S. 15 (1973). The case was decided with four others: *Paris Adult Theater I v. Slaton,* 413 U.S. 49; *U.S.* v. *12 200-Ft. Reels of Super 8mm Film,* 413 U.S. 123; *U.S.* v. *Orito,* 413 U.S. 139; and *Kaplan* v. *California,* 413 U.S. 115.

12. *Miller* v. *California.*

13. Sara Rimer, "Rap Band Members Found Not Guilty in Obscenity Trial," *The New York Times,* Oct. 21, 1990, p. 1.

14. *Pope* v. *Illinois,* No. 85-1973 (1987).

15. *Young* v. *American Mini Theatres, Inc.,* 427 U.S. 50 (1976).

16. Cox, p. 29.

Chapter Eight

1. Ben Bagdikian, quoted in Hentoff, p. 22.

2. *Tinker* v. *Des Moines Independent School District,* 393 U.S. 503 (1969).

3. Ibid.

4. Stuart Taylor, Jr., "Court, 5–3, Widens Power of Schools to Act as Censors," *The New York Times,* January 14, 1988, p. 1.

5. *Hazelwood School District* v. *Kuhlmeier,* 484 U.S. 260 (1988).

6. *The New York Times*, January 15, 1988, p. A30.

7. Hentoff, p. 344.

8. "Student at Brown Is Expelled Under a Rule Barring 'Hate Speech,'" *The New York Times,* February 12, 1991, p. A17.

9. Ibid.

10. Nat Hentoff, "Free Speech on Campus," *The Progressive* (May 1989), reprinted in Orr, pp. 148–53.

11. Richard Bernstein, "Opening the Books on Censorship," *The New York Times Magazine,* May 13, 1984, p. 36.

12. Bernstein, p. 91.

13. Peter Scales, "Sex, Psychology, and Censorship," *The Humanist* (July/August 1987), reprinted in Orr, p. 127.

14. Linda Greenhouse, "High Court Limits Banning of Books," *The New York Times,* June 26, 1982, p. 1.

15. Phyllis Schlafly, "Citizens' Bill of Rights About Schools and

Libraries," *The Phyllis Schlafly Report* (February 1983), re-printed in Orr, pp. 134–35.

16. American Library Association, "Freedom to Read," reprinted in Orr, pp. 137–39.
17. ALA, op. cit., in Orr, p. 139.

Chapter Nine

1. *The New York Times*, November 22, 1991, p. A30.
2. Anthony Lewis, "How Freedom Died," *The New York Times,* November 22, 1991, p. A31.
3. McClosky and Brill, pp. 48–92.
4. Milton, op. cit.
5. Arthur Goldberg, address delivered at Western Connecticut State University, April 23, 1980; text reprinted in *The* (WCSU) *Echo,* April 29, 1980.
6. Earl Warren, *A Republic, If You Can Keep It* (New York: Quad-rangle Books, 1972), pp. 168–69.
7. William Pitt, speech on the India Bill, November 1783.

For Further
Information

Recommended Reading

Bach, Julie S., ed. *Civil Liberties: Opposing Viewpoints.* San Diego: Greenhaven Press, 1988.

Bernards, Neal, ed. *The Mass Media: Opposing Viewpoints.* San Diego: Greenhaven Press, 1988.

Burress, Lee. *Battle of the Books: Literary Censorship in the Public Schools.* Metuchen, N.J.: Scarecrow Press, 1989.

Demac, Donna. *Liberty Denied: The Current Rise of Censorship in America.* New York: PEN American Center, 1988.

Douglas, William O. *The Right of the People.* New York: Doubleday, 1958.

Emery, Edwin. *The Press and America: An Interpretive History of the Mass Media.* Englewood Cliffs, N.J.: Prentice-Hall, 1972.

Forer, Lois G. *A Chilling Effect: The Mounting Threat of Libel and Invasion of Privacy Actions to the First Amendment.* New York: W. W. Norton, 1987.

Friendly, Fred W. *The Constitution—That Delicate Balance.* New York: Random House, 1984.

Haskel, Claudia, and Jean H. Otto, eds. *A Time for Choices.* Denver, Colo.: The First Amendment Congress, 1991.

Hentoff, Nat. *The First Freedom: The Tumultuous History of Free Speech in America.* New York: Delacorte Press, 1988.

Kronenwetter, Michael. *Free Press v. Fair Trial.* New York: Franklin Watts, 1986.

Kupferman, Theodore R. *Censorship, Secrecy, Access, and Obscenity.* Westport, Conn.: Meckler, 1990.

Meltzer, Milton. *The Bill of Rights: How We Got It and What It Means.* New York: Thomas Y. Crowell, 1990.

Orr, Lisa, ed. *Censorship: Opposing Viewpoints.* San Diego: Greenhaven Press, 1990.

Rhodehamel, John H., et. al. *Foundations of Freedom.* Los Angeles: Constitutional Rights Foundation, 1991.

Rogers, Donald J. *Banned! Book Censorship in the Schools.* New York: Messner, 1988.

Trager, Oliver. *The Arts and Media in America: Freedom or Censorship?* New York: Facts On File, 1991.

Warren, Earl. *A Republic, If You Can Keep It.* New York: Quadrangle Books, 1972.

Weiss, Ann E. *Who's to Know? Information, the Media, and Public Awareness.* Boston: Houghton Mifflin, 1990.

Zerman, Melvin Bernard. *Taking On the Press: Constitutional Rights in Conflict.* New York: Thomas Y. Crowell, 1986.

Organizations to Contact:

American Civil Liberties Union, 132 W. 43rd St., New York, NY 10036

American Library Association, 50 E. Huron St., Chicago, IL 60611

Constitutional Rights Foundation, 601 S. Kingsley Dr., Los Angeles, CA 90005

First Amendment Congress, University of Colorado at Denver, Graduate School of Public Affairs, 1445 Market St., Suite 320, Denver, CO 80202

Gannett Foundation, 1101 Wilson Blvd., Arlington, VA 22209

PEN American Center, 568 Broadway, New York, NY 10012

People for the American Way, 2000 M St., Suite 400, Washington, DC 20036

Reporters Committee for Freedom of the Press, 1735 Eye St. NW, Washington, DC 20006

Index

(126)